Martin Luther

ON THE
FREEDOM
OF A CHRISTIAN

With Related Texts

D1563368

Martin Luther

ON THE
FREEDOM
OF A CHRISTIAN

With Related Texts

Edited and Translated, with an Introduction, by
Tryntje Helfferich

Hackett Publishing Company, Inc.
Indianapolis/Cambridge

For further information, please address
          Hackett Publishing Company, Inc.
          P.O. Box 44937
          Indianapolis, Indiana 46244-0937

          www.hackettpublishing.com

Cover design by Abigail Coyle
Interior design by Elizabeth L. Wilson
Composition by Aptara, Inc.

Library of Congress Cataloging-in-Publication Data

Luther, Martin, 1483–1546.
   [Tractatus de libertate Christiana. English]
   The freedom of a Christian: with related texts / Martin Luther; edited and
translated with an introduction by Tryntje Helfferich.
       pages cm
   Includes bibliographical references and index.
   ISBN 978-0-87220-768-4 (pbk.) — ISBN 978-0-87220-767-7 (cloth)
   1. Liberty—Religious aspects—Christianity. I. Helfferich, Tryntje, 1969–
editor of compilation. II. Title.
   BR 332.S6L88 2013
   233'.7—dc23   2013017633

The paper used in this publication meets the minimum requirements of
American National Standard for Information Sciences—Permanence of Paper
for Printed Library Materials, ANSI Z39.48–1984.

Contents

I. General Introduction

In the year 1520, when Martin Luther wrote *On the Freedom of a Christian*, Europe was divided. It was politically fragmented, split into numerous competing and often hostile kingdoms and states; socially and economically stratified, with some people possessing vast influence and wealth, some living in thriving cities, and the majority working to eke out a subsistence living through farming; and also dissimilar by many other measures, such as language, dress, customs, and forms of government. Among intellectuals, moreover, there was vigorous disagreement over the nature of the world, humanity, and humanity's relationship to the divine. Yet in one key way in the year 1520, Europe was comparatively united. Other than a few groups of religious radicals and the scattered communities of Jews, there was general agreement that the Holy Catholic Church was the one true church, that the pope was its head, that only through the church could one achieve salvation, and that the church was responsible for the final determinations of both religious doctrine and practice. Church traditions, ceremonies, strictures, laws, and observances shaped the way people led their daily lives, shaped the calendar, shaped politics, law, family life, university curricula, and even understandings of such fundamental human experiences as suffering and death. Indeed, Europeans saw themselves as being a part not of Europe but of Christendom.

Very soon after 1520, however, this relative religious unanimity was lost. As a result of the revolutionary movements of Martin Luther and other reformers, Europeans as a whole still believed in God and Christ, but the influence of the church had changed. Instead of one religious authority and one broad range of accepted orthodox understandings of Christianity and Scripture, European spiritual foundations had ruptured and Christians now followed various competing religious authorities, each with profoundly different and even conflicting understandings of the nature of the Christian faith and each with different teachings on appropriate Christian practice, Christian life, and the relationship between church and state. War was the unfortunate result, and only after 1648, following decades of confusion, chaos, and violent bloodshed leaving many millions dead, would people come to a grudging acceptance of this new religious diversity. Luther's *On the Freedom of a Christian* was just one small part of this dramatic change in the life of Europeans, but it presented perhaps the clearest and most influential statement of the principles driving the early Reformation era. "Faith alone," Luther argued, "without any works, makes one pious, free, and saved."[1] With this simple formulation, he challenged the teachings and authority of the old church while simultaneously laying out the blueprint for a new one. To understand the Reformation and the vast changes it engendered, in other words, *On the Freedom of a Christian* is a good place to start.

The Life of Martin Luther

Martin Luther was born in 1483 in the small mining town of Eisleben, in the county of Mansfeld, which was in turn one of hundreds of counties, duchies, principalities, and free cities contained within the Holy Roman Empire. This empire, which sprawled across much of central Europe, was seen by many contemporary political theorists as a direct descendent of the ancient Roman Empire, but in practice it owed more to Charlemagne and his later Germanic descendants than it did to Augustus Caesar. Lacking a strong central authority, it was instead a composite state, a decentralized political body ruled by an emperor who did not inherit his position, but was elected by the seven greatest imperial princes, known as electors. Among these was Frederick the Wise of Saxony, Mansfeld's mightiest neighbor, who was named elector in 1486 and who would later become one of Luther's most influential supporters. Frederick was a man brimming with religious enthusiasm, not only undertaking a pilgrimage to Jerusalem in 1493, but also becoming a passionate collector of holy relics, which soon filled his castle in Wittenberg by the thousands. In 1502, eager to demonstrate his sophistication and power, Frederick

---

1. Luther, *On the Freedom of a Christian*, §8.

also founded a new university at Wittenberg, with faculties in the fields of theology, law, and medicine. He was aided in both his collecting and his academic patronage by the great wealth he drew from the copper and silver mines found within his territories, and from the profit he collected when these metals were formed into new coins for circulation.

At the time of Luther's birth, Saxony, the Holy Roman Empire, and Europe as a whole were undergoing significant changes. The recent rise of a monetary economy and new market forces had enriched men like Frederick, but had also coincided with inflationary pressures, the flourishing and increasing prosperity of the cities, rapid popula- tion growth in the countryside, and a new social mobility. Rural life- styles and food production, moreover, were being affected both by land shortages and by the unpredictable and colder weather patterns of the time, which caused uncertainty and led to a series of famines and food shortages.[2] Politically there were further changes, as rulers in this period (both within the empire and without) were attempting to cen- tralize their power at the expense of localities, stripping from local com- munities the tools of self-rule that they believed to be their right. Rulers did this through the creation of new and ever-larger bureaucracies and the introduction of the old Roman legal code, which gave them greater influence over their people than they had ever previously enjoyed.

In the intellectual realm, the ideas of the Renaissance and renewed interest in classical and early Christian writings had spurred the devel- opment of a new intellectual movement, humanism, which matched an enthusiasm for ancient documentary sources with a disappointment over what humanists saw as the petty corruption and excessive formal- ism of the modern church. Humanist philosophy would become quite popular in the late fifteenth and early sixteenth centuries, but was only one of a handful of orthodox intellectual movements then flourishing within the universities.

Thomists, for example, who were followers of the philosophy of St. Thomas Aquinas (1225–1274), argued in favor of the *via antiqua* (old way), which posited that the natural world, church doctrines, and divine

---

2. For more on the climate in this period, see Brian Fagan, *The Little Ice Age: How Climate Made History, 1300–1850* (New York: Basic Books, 2001).

truths could be explained using a combination of human reason and Scripture. God, they also argued, gave humans the gift of faith, but this faith was not salvific unless one, moved by God's grace, then voluntarily assented to it and perfected it through love for God and one's neighbor.

Ockhamists, sometimes called nominalists, were followers of William of Ockham (c. 1288–c. 1347) and advocates of the competing *via moderna* (new way). This philosophy elevated God's majesty and stressed human limitations, and it posited that reason and logic could explain the natural world, but knowledge of the divine must be gained through inner experience and faith alone. Ockhamists argued further that Christians, unable to penetrate the mind of God or fully know His will, must nevertheless strive to conform to His commandments to the best of their ability; only then would God's grace and mercy set them on the path of performing the meritorious works that eventually made them worthy of eternal life.

A third, somewhat less popular school of thought was modern Augustinianism. Proponents of this theology argued, following St. Augustine of Hippo (354–430), that all humans were irreparably stained by the original sin of Adam and Eve, and were thus incapable of fulfilling God's law and unworthy of salvation. Thus unlike Thomists and Ockhamists, who believed that humans possessed free will and could cooperate in their own salvation, modern Augustinians argued that human depravity and selfishness ensured that no one could ever work toward or earn justification, which must instead be an unwarranted gift of divine acceptance. Even within these schools, however, philosophers often disagreed, and a vigorous exchange of ideas took place both within and across all the late-medieval intellectual traditions.

While the university professors argued finer points of theology, Europeans in general had responded to their chaotic, unpredictable, and changeable world by an unprecedented religiosity and search for divine comfort and assurance of salvation. Especially after the mid-fourteenth century and the horrors of the Black Death, which had led to a pervasive fear of death, damnation, and the devil, religious enthusiasm had pushed Christians into ever-greater participation in church rituals and rites, and had driven them in large numbers to undertake pilgrimages, collect holy relics, worship at shrines of the saints, join religious confraternities, make bequests to the church, meditate on Christ's passion, and vigorously undertake all manner of religious activity either mediated or unmediated by church officials. A widespread belief in the imminent end of days and the second coming of Christ, a belief heightened by the growing existential threat to Christendom posed by the Ottoman Turks after the mid-fifteenth century, further spurred the faithful into extraordinary acts of pious devotion out of fear of God's wrath and Christ's terrible and inexorable judgment. "He will say to those at His left hand," the Book of Matthew warned, "'You that are accursed, depart from Me into the eternal fire prepared for the devil and his angels.'" But those who were righteous should not despair, for Christ "will say to those at His right hand, 'Come, you that are blessed by My Father, inherit the kingdom prepared for you from the foundation of the world.'"[3] By the time of Luther's birth, the religiosity sparked by this combination of deathly fear and desperate hope had allowed the church to become extremely influential and powerful—and the largest landholder in Europe.

Yet despite its successes, the late-fifteenth-century church was also struggling to meet some substantial challenges. Open criticism of its bureaucratic inflexibility, notorious instances of high-level corruption, and squabbling between popes and church councils, for example, had left the leaders of the church defensive and sensitive to perceived challenges to their authority. Furthermore, such everyday abuses as concubinage and immorality among the common clergy, simony (the sale of church offices), and clerical absenteeism and pluralism (the holding of multiple church offices) stubbornly resisted eradication and were loudly condemned by humanists and many others. Clerical ignorance, ongoing public quarrels among priests and monks, and widespread popular resentment of both the special privileges afforded the clergy and the church's great wealth further contributed to a widespread anticlericalism. In his *Praise of Folly* (1511), for example, the famed Dutch humanist Desiderius Erasmus criticized the leaders of the church for their focus on secular wealth and power, while "the care of the sheep they either commend to Christ Himself or pass on to their brothers,

---

3. Matt. 25:41, 25:34.

as they call them, and [to the] vicars. They don't so much as remember
their own name—what the word 'bishop' means—namely, painstaking
labor and concern. But in casting their nets for money, there they play
the bishop, and keep a sharp enough lookout."[4] Even the extreme religiosity of the people, Erasmus and others argued, was not necessarily a
sign of the health of Christian society, for popular practice often degenerated into little more than superstition, idolatry, and belief in magical
charms. Given such arguments and the sheer complexity and variety of
late-fifteenth-century religious life, modern scholars (many influenced
by their own religious viewpoints) have been entirely unable to agree
whether the church was remarkably healthy, popular, and exuberant at
the time of Martin Luther's birth, or rotten, decadent, and stagnant.[5]

Martin's father, Hans Luther, was a product of the new social
mobility that was then transforming the empire and the rest of western Europe. Born a peasant, he had left the farm to become a copper miner and mine owner, wealthy and ambitious enough to pay for
an education for his son, who he hoped might become a lawyer and
further advance the family's fortunes. Young Martin was a willing student, entering the University of Erfurt in 1501 and receiving a master's degree in 1505. He then began his studies of the law, but almost
immediately dropped out and joined a local Augustinian monastery.
His father was furious. Only later did Luther explain that he had been
caught in a violent thunderstorm and, in fear of death and the judgment of God, had taken a vow to Saint Anne, the patron saint of miners, that he would become a monk if only he might survive.

Whatever the reason for Luther's sudden decision, he then dedicated himself to his new calling, scrupulously following the many
regulations of the Augustinian order for a life of strict discipline and

---

4. Desiderius Erasmus, *The Praise of Folly*, trans. Clarence H. Miller, 2nd ed.
(New Haven, CT: Yale University Press, 2003), 110. The word "bishop" comes
from the Greek *episcopos*, which means overseer or guardian.

5. See for example the discussions over the nature of the pre-Reformation
English church in A. G. Dickens, *The English Reformation*, 2nd ed. (University
Park, PA: Pennsylvania State Press, 1989) and Eamon Duffy, *The Stripping of the
Altars: Traditional Religion in England, 1400–1580*, 2nd ed. (New Haven, CT:
Yale University Press, 2005).

simplicity, punctuated by frequent prayers at fixed times throughout the day based on the canonical hours. Plagued by doubt about his worthiness before God, however, Luther became deeply depressed and fearful, and so pushed himself ever harder to grow in humility and please God through additional prayers, fasting, and frequent confessions of his sins to the head of his order, his friend and confessor Johannes von Staupitz. Yet none of this seemed sufficient, and, convinced of his damnation, he began to fear and hate God. In such a state of mind "God appears horrifyingly angry," he wrote some time later, "and with Him the whole creation. There can be no flight, nor consolation either from within or from without, but all is accusation."[6]

In 1507 Luther was ordained into the priesthood, and in the next year, partly to distract Luther, but also to take advantage of his obvious intelligence, Staupitz sent him to the new University of Wittenberg to study theology. He earned his doctorate there in October 1512 and was named a professor. Though he had studied the works of Aristotle, of such renowned theologians as Peter Lombard, William of Ockham, and Gabriel Biel, and of Luther's contemporary Erasmus, his special and fervent interest was in the Bible itself, and this (especially lectures on the Psalms and the letters of Paul) now became the focus of his teaching. By 1515 he was also serving as a district vicar and preaching at the Wittenberg town church, and was thus heavily engaged both in the university and in the local community. Indeed, it was his local parishioners who first brought to his attention the sale of indulgences in neighboring towns and villages.

Martin Luther's Ideas in the Context of Sixteenth-Century Theology and Church Practice

According to the teachings of the church, sin was thought to have two consequences, or punishments: eternal and temporal. Eternal punishment was God's retribution for mortal sin, and it damned the sinner to hell. Yet medieval theologians taught that contrite Christians could have the guilt and responsibility for this eternal punishment

---

6. E. G. Rupp and B. Drewery, eds., *Martin Luther* (London, 1970), 5.

absolved or forgiven by the church. This absolution was thought possible because, through God's mercy, Christ had given this power to the apostles and through them to the priests. Cited as proof of this were biblical passages such as John 20:22–23: "And when He had said this, He breathed on them, and said to them, 'Receive the Holy Spirit. If you forgive the sins of any, they are forgiven; if you retain the sins of any, they are retained.'" While the church rejected the idea that one could then avoid hell and achieve salvation solely through one's own efforts (a heresy known as Pelagianism), the majority of theologians argued that faith (seen as a gift from God) must be accompanied by acts or works that helped the sinner qualify for God's grace. The most important of these acts were termed sacraments, which were church ceremonies that served as outward signs indicating the imparting of inward divine grace or favor.

The sacrament of baptism was performed during one's infancy and was seen as essential for salvation. Through baptism, the Christian was freed from the guilt of original sin (the sin of Adam that was thought to be inherited by all humans). Subsequent sins required the sacrament of penance (or confession), which every Christian was required to perform at least once a year. This allowed the believer to have his eternal punishment for these new sins absolved, and so gave him renewed access to God's grace and the hope of salvation. A third sacrament, the Mass or Eucharist, was central to medieval Christian worship and was thus a large part of the believer's experience of the church. As a sacrament, the Mass was thought to help the Christian gain God's grace, but it was also seen as a representation of the last supper of Christ, a sacrifice to God, a reminder of Christ's sacrifice and offering of eternal life, and a means of communion or spiritual union with God. Other sacraments included confirmation, the taking of holy orders, marriage, and last rites (or extreme unction). These, along with other acts of piety, charity, and devotion, were then the key means by which the believer could acquire or cooperate with divine grace and so help himself gain God's love.

The second consequence of sin was temporal punishment, which was separate from eternal punishment and which an absolved sinner was still required to satisfy in order to account for the offence committed against God by sin. This punishment was thus both an act of reparation required to bring the sinner back into friendship with God, and an act to hinder the further commission of sin. Any temporal punishment not served in this lifetime was thought to carry over into the afterlife, for the sinner would be required to satisfy it in the excruciating fires of purgatory before he could be granted entry into heaven. Here too, however, the church argued that it could aid the contrite sinner through the acts of satisfaction (or penance) imposed by the confessor during the sacrament of penance. Those living could also aid the passage of the dead from purgatory through the offering of masses and prayers. Yet the church could only estimate the amount of work necessary for satisfaction; God alone knew the precise temporal punishment due for sin. Furthermore, although confessors tried to aid the faithful in a searching analysis of their consciences during the sacrament of penance, even a good Christian could never be confident that he had fully confessed and absolved all his sins. Thus he could never know if he had properly paid his debt to God and could never be assured salvation. This was Martin Luther's problem, and so the sacraments offered him little solace, instead filling him, and others of his time, with an agony of self-doubt, anxiety, and terror. If only there was more that could be done to earn God's grace!

To meet this need within Christian society, to mitigate or replace some of the more extreme and often harsh prescriptions for public penance of the early medieval period, and to reward great displays of piety or charity, over time the church had developed a process of granting indulgences. An indulgence was, simply stated, the remittance of the temporal punishment required for sins whose guilt had already been absolved or forgiven. While ordinary sinners struggled to make reparation to God, the theologians argued, Christ and the saints had possessed overwhelming and indeed superabundant merit or goodness far in excess of anything they had required for entry into heaven. This treasury of merit, as it was known, was thought to be something the church could then tap for the benefit of humanity, for according to the Bible, the successors of the apostle Peter (i.e., the popes) had been granted the keys to the kingdom of heaven by Christ (Matt. 16:18–19). By an act of divine goodness or suffrage, therefore, God had allowed the church another way to help the contrite sinner discharge his debt to God.

While the indulgence system had the beneficial effect of encouraging acts of devotion and piety, it was also subject to enormous abuses. Indulgences offered for sale without requiring contrition or prayer, indulgences offering thousands of years off theoretical time in purgatory, indulgences offering absolution from or forgiveness of sin (which could only be granted through the sacrament of penance), and even indulgences promising a direct trip to heaven all appeared and were denounced by church officials. Humanists such as Erasmus also roundly criticized the sale of indulgences. "Imagine here, if you please," he wrote in his *Praise of Folly*, "some businessman or soldier or judge who thinks that if he throws into the collection basket one coin from all his plunder, the whole cesspool of his sinful life will be immediately wiped out. He thinks all his acts of perjury, lust, drunkenness, quarreling, murder, deception, dishonesty, betrayal are paid off like a mortgage, and paid off in such a way that he can start off once more on a whole new round of sinful pleasures."[7] And still such corruptions were all too common and were almost impossible to stamp out given both the enormous religious enthusiasm that was a hallmark of the era and the difficulty of the theological underpinnings of the entire system.

In 1517, Pope Leo X authorized the issuance of indulgences to those good Christians who gave alms for rebuilding St. Peter's Basilica in Rome—a project that would require enormous sums (and that would create what today is recognized as one of the finest buildings in the world). Due to the complex politics of the day, however, no indulgences were to be offered within the territory of the elector of Saxony, including Luther's home city of Wittenberg. Yet indulgences were readily available just over the border, and a number of Luther's parishioners eagerly traveled the short distance in order to acquire one. The stories they told on their return appalled Luther, for he could not believe the corruption. The official tasked by the church to oversee the issuance of indulgences in that area, the Dominican friar Johann Tetzel, was

---

7. Erasmus, *The Praise of Folly*, 64–65.

seemingly so eager to raise funds that he was simply selling the indulgences: a cold financial transaction with no thought as to the spiritual status or contrition of the buyer. Even worse, some of Luther's parishioners had become convinced that with one of Tetzel's indulgences they could purchase the instant release of their dead relatives from purgatory, or, if the indulgence was for themselves, that they would receive instant absolution for all past and future sins upon receipt.

Luther's *Ninety-Five Theses on the Power and Efficacy of Indulgences*,[8] which he wrote in Latin and posted at the castle church in Wittenberg on 31 October 1517, not only expressed concern over such abuses, but implicitly called into question the entire indulgence system and sacrament of penance. Though designed simply to elicit discussion among local academics and not revolutionary in itself, the *Ninety-Five Theses* was the first step in Luther's eventual break with the church, and 31 October is celebrated as Reformation Day in many Lutheran areas today. Within weeks a copy of the *Ninety-Five Theses* had been sent to the pope, and within months the document had been translated into German and published, with copies of it in both Latin and vernacular languages appearing throughout Europe.

Luther had hoped to bring to light abuses within the church and to spark a conversation among churchmen over the proper nature and practice of Christian repentance, but church officials, stung by Luther's apparent questioning of the church's right to set doctrine, responded by reasserting papal power and demanding Luther's retraction and recantation. Numerous efforts were made to bring Luther to heel, yet every time the church pushed Luther to submit, it had the opposite effect of radicalizing him. Thus by 1518, after a collegial meeting at Heidelberg with Staupitz and other Augustinians, and then a much more unpleasant meeting at Augsburg with the papal legate Cardinal Thomas Cajetan (which degenerated into a violent argument), Luther was not only attacking the entire system of indulgences, he was also

---

8. Martin Luther, *D. Martin Luthers Werke: Kritische Gesamtausgabe*, vol. 1 (Weimar: H. Böhlau, 1883), 233–39. For the controversy over whether Luther actually posted the theses, rather than simply mailing a copy to Archbishop Albrecht of Mainz, see Joachim Ott and Martin Treu, eds., *Luthers Thesenanschlag—Faktum oder Fiktion?* (Leipzig: Evangelische Verlagsanstalt, 2008).

openly espousing sweeping new ideas about such fundamental concepts as justification, the nature of mankind, and free will.

It is difficult to determine exactly when and how Luther's philosophical shift had occurred. Many years later, in the 1545 preface to
a complete edition of his Latin writings, Luther himself described his
breakthrough. It came, he recalled, while he contemplated one verse
in the letters of St. Paul to the Romans: "For in it the righteousness of
God is revealed through faith for faith; as it is written, 'He who through
faith is righteous shall live'" (Romans 1:17). This passage had always
filled him with dread. "I hated that word 'righteousness of God,'" he
wrote, "which, according to the use and custom of all the teachers, I
had been taught to understand philosophically regarding the formal or
active righteousness, as they called it, with which God is righteous and
punishes the unrighteous sinner."[9] Yet after deep contemplation, medi-
tation, and "by the mercy of God," he continued, "I began to understand
that the righteousness of God is that by which the righteous lives by a
gift of God, namely by faith. And this is the meaning: the righteousness of God is revealed by the gospel, namely, the passive righteousness
with which merciful God justifies us by faith, as it is written, 'He who
through faith is righteous shall live.' Here I felt that I was altogether
born again and had entered paradise itself through open gates. There a
totally other face of the entire Scripture showed itself to me."[10]

This reconception of God's righteousness was at the heart of
Luther's entire theology, which was mostly in place by 1518 and which
he would then develop over time. Luther argued that Christ's righteousness is merely imputed to humans, and not because of anything they
do. This was in contradiction to the standard late-medieval conception
that humankind is infused with and gradually transformed by God's
grace through participation in the sacraments and the performance of
acts of charity and other good works. One cooperated in one's own salvation, for the believer who acquired the habit of doing good would
indeed become good over time. As the Ockhamist theologian Gabriel

---

9. J. Pelikan and H. Lehmann, eds., *Luther's Works* [hereafter cited as LW], vol.
34 (St. Louis, MO and Philadelphia: Concordia/Fortress Press, 1960), 336–37.
10. Ibid.

Biel wrote: "God has established the rule [covenant] that whoever turns to Him and does what he can, will receive forgiveness of sin from God. God infuses assisting grace into such a man, who is thus taken back into friendship."[11] Luther, however, argued that God ascribes Christ's righteousness to humans, covers them with it as a free gift. Righteousness is thus passive, not active, and it does not change people internally, but comes from the outside and is foreign. "Later," Luther noted, "I read Augustine's *The Spirit and the Letter* where contrary to hope I found that he, too, interpreted God's righteousness in a similar way, as the righteousness with which God clothes us when He justifies us."[12]

Strongly influenced by his reading of St. Augustine, Luther argued that humans are utterly unworthy of this gift, and nothing they do— no good works, no following of God's law, no participation in rituals, sacraments, or ceremonies—could possibly ever make them worthy. Only through God's gift of grace, which is faith in Him, can they be saved, "for faith alone justifies us and fulfils the law," Luther argued, "and this because faith brings us the Spirit gained by the merits of Christ. The Spirit in turn gives us the happiness and freedom at which the law aims."[13] Such faith is not something people can choose to do or have, but is God's righteousness itself, which appears in the believer as "a living and unshakable confidence, a belief in the grace of God so assured that a man would die a thousand deaths for its sake."[14] God gives the believer this faith for the sake of Christ, who willingly and voluntarily took upon Himself humanity's sins and died on the cross, thus giving the believer an unearned righteousness and freeing him from sin and death.

On the one hand, this view is a terrifying loss of control; the believer has no ability to save himself, no free will, but is utterly at the mercy of God. On the other hand, this view is incredibly freeing;

---

11. Heiko Oberman, ed., *Forerunners of the Reformation: The Shape of Late Medieval Thought* (Cambridge, 1966), 173.

12. LW 34:338.

13. Preface to Luther's *Commentary on the Epistle to the Romans* from Bertram Lee Woolf, ed., *The Reformation Writings of Martin Luther*, vol. 2 (London: Philosophical Library, 1956), 286.

14. Ibid., 289.

the believer knows that God does not require his works to save him, and He does so simply out of mercy and love. In developing these ideas, which are sometimes termed the doctrines of *sola gratia* (grace alone) and *sola fide* (faith alone), Luther firmly rejected the entire sacramental system of the church. (He retained the word "sacrament," applying it to baptism and communion, but redefined its meaning into something entirely different.) Another important idea of Luther's, sometimes termed *sola scriptura* (Scripture alone), similarly challenged the church's claims to authority. Here Luther argued that the church had fraudulently usurped power over Christians, and that Scripture alone was the final authority for all matters of faith and Christian practice. With one blow, this argument (which echoed the teaching of the early-fifteenth-century Bohemian reformer and heretic Jan Hus) contradicted the dominant philosophical view that church traditions, the writings of church fathers, the decrees of church councils and popes, and the laws and regulations established by the church over the centuries should be considered authoritative. Furthermore, Luther argued, Christians did not need a priesthood to mediate for them with God. Each man was his own priest and the overseer of his own soul.

Martin Luther's Friends and Opponents

Determined to counter Luther's ideas, which he believed to be heretical, in 1518 the German theologian Johannes Eck (1486–1543) challenged Luther's close supporter and colleague Andreas Bodenstein von Karlstadt (1486–1541) to a public disputation at Leipzig. This debate began in June 1519, and Luther himself, who was present, soon took Karlstadt's place. Here Luther forcefully defended his theological ideas, but, pushed ever harder by Eck, now also publicly repudiated the power and authority of both the papacy and church councils, and admitted the similarity of his ideas with those of Hus. The Leipzig debate would thus be a key point in convincing Luther that a break with Rome was inevitable. The debate also cemented Eck as one of Luther's principal Catholic opponents in the years to come, and certainly one of the most prolific and popular. By the end of his life Eck had printed scores of books and pamphlets critical of Luther's teaching, and had established his reputation as the most vociferous defender of the Catholic Church in the Reformation era. After Leipzig, Eck was also instrumental in pushing Pope Leo X to issue a special papal bull (or edict) titled *Exsurge Domine* (Arise O Lord), which banned Luther's writings and threatened him with excommunication if he did not recant. Luther refused, marking his opposition by ceremoniously burning copies of the bull and other church writings in a bonfire outside the gates of Wittenberg. On 3 January 1521 the pope thus issued a formal ban of excommunication.

In the year before this final and irreparable break with the church, Luther had been hard at work spreading his ideas. This he did both through lectures at Wittenberg and through publications designed to reach a far broader audience. Indeed, three of Luther's most famous works appeared during this time of enormous uncertainty. The first, written in German, was *Address to the Christian Nobility of the German Nation*. It challenged the power of the church over the secular realm, appealed to the imperial princes to rectify the errors of the papacy, denied the sole authority of the pope to elucidate Scripture, and rejected the idea that the pope alone could call general church councils. Next came *On the Babylonian Captivity of the Church*, which denied the validity of the current sacramental system, redefined the very meaning of the sacraments, attacked the theology of the Mass, argued for a "priesthood of all believers," and accused the pope of being the Antichrist. Finally came *On the Freedom of a Christian*, which was published in late 1520, and which laid out Luther's conception of what it meant to be a Christian and to live a Christian life. These three booklets were incredibly popular, bringing Luther thousands of new followers, and were reprinted across Europe. Yet none of these writings did anything to win Luther support among the firm church faithful. On the contrary, some who had initially supported his calls for reform were now repelled. Erasmus, for example, a moderate who shared some ideas with Luther and had at first refused to denounce him, now became disenchanted by Luther's intemperate attacks on free will and by his willingness to destroy church unity in the name of doctrinal purity.

Within the political realm, Luther depended on the support of his patron, Elector Frederick the Wise, who convinced Emperor Charles

V to hold off on implementing the ban of excommunication against Luther until he was given a proper hearing. This occurred at the imperial diet (or general assembly) held at the city of Worms in 1521, but the result was not what Luther had hoped. Instead of allowing Luther to convince him of the rightness of his position, the emperor merely offered Luther another opportunity to recant. Luther refused and so was named a heretic, outlaw, and enemy of the empire. Aided again by Frederick of Saxony, Luther then went into hiding at Wartburg Castle in Eisenach. Living under an assumed name and in constant fear of the devil and uncertainty over his future, Luther nevertheless continued his work, producing among other things a translation into German of the New Testament.

Back at Wittenberg, Luther's teachings were continued by his young, brilliant colleague, the humanist scholar Philipp Melanchthon (1497–1560). Melanchthon, a professor of Greek and Hebrew, was a much more systematic thinker than Luther, and in 1521 he composed a fundamental statement of Lutheran principles, published under the title *Loci Communes* (Commonplaces), which Luther praised as a work of theology second only to the Bible itself. Melanchthon would also later be famous for crafting the 1530 Augsburg Confession, a formulation that would become Lutheranism's primary statement of faith. Where Luther was hot-blooded and often emotional, Melanchthon was moderate and even tempered, and despite some disagreements over the years, the two would form an impressively effective partnership that would last their entire lives.

It was a different matter with another of Luther's early supporters, Karlstadt. During Luther's absence at the Wartburg, Karlstadt, following what he believed to be the clear implications of Luther's teachings, moved to implement his religious reform more completely. He abolished the Catholic Mass in Wittenberg in favor of a new evangelical communion service performed in German, not Latin; allowed the removal and destruction of religious relics and images from local churches; and preached against clerical celibacy and infant baptism. Other supporters of Luther also took his ideas in new directions, including a group known as the Zwickau Prophets, who in late 1521 traveled to Wittenberg from the neighboring area of Zwickau, in

Thuringia. These men, who received some encouragement from Karlstadt and who may have influenced his views on issues such as infant
baptism, also claimed to receive direct new revelations from the Holy
Spirit, which they believed were more authoritative than the Bible, and
which warned them of the imminent end of the world.

The sudden changes made at Wittenberg by Karlstadt, along with
the teachings of the Zwickau Prophets, precipitated a general disorder that now pushed Luther to return from exile. His subsequent sermons denouncing the changes, criticizing the Prophets, and labeling
them and their followers as fanatics shocked and hurt Karlstadt, who
had seen himself as simply fulfilling Luther's teachings. Disillusioned
about Luther and university life, Karlstadt soon left Wittenberg to
serve as a pastor at the neighboring town of Orlamünde, where he
successfully instituted his different and more extreme reform ideas.[15]
Another man likely influenced by the Prophets was Thomas Müntzer
(c. 1490–1525), a scholar and clergyman who was also an early supporter of Luther's and who had spent time in Wittenberg before mov-
ing to Zwickau. Like the Prophets, Müntzer rejected infant baptism
and believed in the superior authority of the Holy Spirit over the Bible.
He was also similarly convinced of the imminent end of days and
necessity of first cleansing the world of unbelievers. This, combined
with his strong sense of the social injustice of the contemporary class
system in the empire, would soon drive him to become one of the leaders and instigators of the great series of peasant uprisings known as the
German Peasants' War (1524–1526).

The excesses and extreme violence of these peasant rebellions,
which were based mostly on existing social, political, and economic
grievances but which also drew on some of the language and ideas of
religious reform, outraged and horrified Luther. Not only had he never
advocated social revolution, but such a thing seemed to violate biblical teachings. He thus openly threw in his lot with the princes of the

---

15. For more on Karlstadt, and in particular his disagreements with Luther
over the Eucharist, see Amy Nelson Burnett, *Karlstadt and the Origins of the
Eucharistic Controversy: A Study of the Circulation of Ideas* (Oxford: Oxford
University Press, 2011). See also Ronald J. Sider, *Andreas Bodenstein Von
Karlstadt: The Development of His Thought 1517–1525* (Leiden: Brill, 1974).

empire, whom he advised should kill any rebel, "for rebellion is not ordinary murder, but is like a great fire that inflames and devastates a land."[16] This the princes did, and in the bloodbath's aftermath some among the common people became disillusioned with Luther and his message. Yet the success of Luther's movement would now depend not so much on the popular diffusion of his teachings, as it had in the beginning, but on the actions of city magistrates and rulers. Such elites would further his reformation by imposing it from above.

During these years Luther had tried to chart a very narrow course, constantly facing challenges from all sides. His greatest opponents were the Catholics, including church officials, theologians such as Eck, ordinary Catholic monks, nuns, and churchgoers, but also political foes such as Emperor Charles V or the English king Henry VIII. But Luther also faced criticism from other reformers, especially radicals such as Müntzer, who wanted to push Luther's reforms much further than he liked and whom he despised with a passion. His relationship with the other leading magisterial reformers (those who, like Luther, accepted the interdependence of church and secular government and who depended on the support of secular magistrates), such as John Calvin in Geneva and Martin Bucer in Strasbourg, was less fraught and generally collegial, but not without sharp theological disagreements that could, as with Ulrich Zwingli in Zurich, intensify into a furious antagonism. To Luther the Bible was clear, and thus the proper nature of the church and of Christian life was also clear, and it frustrated him to no end that not everyone saw it his way.

Note on the Texts and Translations

Martin Luther's *Freedom* gives his understanding of Christian life and Christian salvation, and is thus a fundamental document for understanding the Reformation. Yet alone it lacks vital context, for Luther's teachings were not accepted uncritically by other theologians and reformers, let alone by ordinary people. Instead, both Luther's ideas and the scriptural interpretations on which they were based garnered fevered opposition and often penetrating criticism from people across

---

16. See Luther, *Against the Robbing and Murdering Hordes of Peasants*, below.

the spectrum of contemporary religious belief. In addition to a text of *Freedom* and its associated letter to Pope Leo X, therefore, this volume contains a number of additional documents. As representatives of the greatest number and volume of attacks on Luther are two selections that defend Catholic doctrine and attack Luther and other reformers for violating church teachings, rejecting church authority, and destroying church unity. From Johannes Eck, Luther's greatest opponent, a selection from the *Enchiridion*, a massive work that was unquestionably the most popular attack on Luther written in the sixteenth century; and from the English bishop John Fisher, a sermon giving a taste of the international nature of the theological tempest that Luther raised.

To indicate the divergence of opinions among the many reformers themselves, I then include a selection from Thomas Müntzer's *Highly Provoked Defense.* Although this document never reached a reading audience, it is characteristic of Müntzer's style and clearly shows his belief both that Luther's reforms went nowhere near far enough, and that Luther was just as corrupt as the Catholics he pretended to scorn. In other words, if Luther was a radical in Eck's and Fisher's eyes, he was a conservative in Müntzer's. Yet Luther was not one to sit by quietly when challenged, but was always quick to take up his pen to denounce and skewer his opponents. To indicate this, the final document is Luther's response to what he believed was the misappropriation and distortion of his ideas by rebellious peasants and by Müntzer.

The collection of texts given in this volume should thus provide a sense of the controversy and complexity of the era, and thereby dispel any lingering conception the reader might have that the form or existence of the Protestant Reformation was uncontested, obvious, and inevitable. I hope that after reading these texts, the undergraduate student or interested general reader will have gained a better understanding not just of Martin Luther's *On the Freedom of a Christian*, but also of its reception within the great variety of opinions circulating freely during the tumultuous Reformation era.

Other modern English editions of most of these texts exist, scattered in various places and volumes. For *Freedom*, there are two available English translations of the German version. The first is by Bertram Lee Woolf and appears in his two-volume *Reformation Writings of Martin Luther,* volume 1 (London: Philosophical Library, 1956, reissued 2001), which also includes a translation of the German version of the letter to Pope Leo X. The second and more modern translation of *Freedom* (though without the letter to Pope Leo) is by Philip D. Krey and Peter D. S. Krey. Like Woolf's, it also appears within a much larger volume, *Luther's Spirituality* (New York: Paulist Press, 2007), but unlike Woolf's, it transforms Luther's text to be more gender inclusive. Both are fine translations in different ways, though I disagree with each on various passages and word choices, and hope that my version is both smoother and more faithful to Luther's tone and meaning. For stand-alone English translations of the longer Latin editions of *Freedom* and the letter to Pope Leo, see Martin Luther, *On Christian Liberty,* translated by W. A. Lambert and revised by Harold J. Grimm (Minneapolis: Fortress Press, 2003) and Martin Luther, *The Freedom of a Christian,* translated by Mark D. Tranvik (Minneapolis: Fortress Press, 2008). Luther's *Against the Peasants* is available in English translation (by Charles M. Jacobs) in Martin Luther, *Luther's Works,* edited by Jaroslav Pelikan and H. Lehmann, volume 46 (St. Louis, MO and Philadelphia: Concordia/Fortress Press, 1967).

Only one English-language translation of the Latin version of the *Enchiridion* exists, John Lewis Battles, *Enchiridion of Commonplaces Against Luther and Other Enemies of the Church* (Grand Rapids: Baker, 1979). As far as I can determine, the selection I provide here is thus the only extant translation of the German version. The definitive modern scholarly edition of Eck's Latin version, which takes into account the many alterations Eck made to the text over the years and which includes a good German-language introduction to the work, is Johannes Eck, *Enchiridion locorum communium adversus Lutherum et alios hostes ecclesiae (1525–1543),* edited by Pierre Fraenkel (Münster: Aschendorff, 1979). A published copy of the 1521 English-language sermon by Bishop John Fisher is available in John Fisher, *The English Works of John Fisher* (Berlin: Asher & Co., 1876). In my offering of this text, I modernized spelling and punctuation to assist the modern reader, but otherwise left it mostly as written.

Müntzer's *Highly Provoked Defense* appears in English translation in two modern collections of texts: Michael G. Baylor, editor and translator, *The Radical Reformation* (Cambridge: Cambridge University Press, 1991); and Peter Matheson, editor and translator, *The Collected Works of Thomas Müntzer* (Edinburgh: T & T Clark, 1988). Both translations are quite different from each other, and from mine. This is unsurprising, as this Müntzer document is devilishly tricky, and occasionally requires the translator to read between the lines to discern meaning, or to take an educated guess about missing words. In the end, I feel my version is somewhat more readable and closer to Müntzer's intended meaning than the others, but I leave the final judgment to my readers.

While three of the texts provided here were originally printed in both Latin and German, the Latin versions were intended solely for a learned audience of theologians, churchmen, and the small number of Latin-educated nobles and urban elites. The German versions were designed to appeal to the common man and thus to expand dramatically the reach of the authors' ideas. Johannes Eck, for example, in the preface to his German version of the *Enchiridion*, explained that he had received numerous appeals and pleas from both "great and humble" people within the empire for a less expensive German-language version of his weighty Latin tome. Such a thing would be, they told him, "not only useful, but, for many reasons, necessary." And he had obliged, "so that the common laity and others who are not skilled in Latin have something with which they might preserve and safeguard themselves against the errors and heresies of the new sects."[17]

Though Eck's Latin *Enchiridion*, in the end, was published in far more editions than his German, vernacular-language texts were generally much more widely read and influential than Latin ones. As this volume is not intended for the theologian or advanced Reformation scholar (who would at any rate undoubtedly read the texts in their original languages), it seemed reasonable for consistency's sake to offer here translations of the three German-language versions that would

---

17. Johannes Eck, *Enchiridion, Handbüchlin gemainer stell unnd Artickel der jetzt schwebenden Neuwen leeren*, Faksimile-Druck der Ausgabe (Augsburg 1533), edited by Erwin Iserloh (Münster: Aschendorff, 1980), 2.

have been available to any literate reader of the era. The decision to offer the German version of the *Enchiridion* was made easier, as well, by the glaring lack of any existing English translation to date. Note however that sixteenth-century German, especially in the style written by theologians, is sometimes extremely difficult to translate into readable modern English. I have tried to stay as true to the original texts as possible, deviating only when necessary for comprehension and seeking always to maintain consistency in the translation of key terms. It is also purely for ease of comprehension that I follow the more old-fashioned style of capitalizing all pronouns referring to the divine.

Acknowledgments

My great thanks to Amy R. Caldwell, Grant Weyburne, Nancy McLoughlin, and Carla Helfferich for assisting in the preparation of this text and for double-checking my introductions and translations for readability.

II. The Freedom of a Christian

Introduction

In 1520 Luther produced three major works that would define his new interpretation of Christian doctrine and authority. They would also help spur a religious, political, and social revolution in Europe. These three treatises, *Address to the Christian Nobility of the German Nation*, *On the Babylonian Captivity of the Church*, and *On the Freedom of a Christian*, clearly and powerfully express Luther's ideas that the church was corrupt, its leaders morally and spiritually bankrupt, and its doctrines criminally mistaken. Of these three works, the last was the least inflammatory in its language against the papacy and focused not so much on tearing down the existing church as in building up an explanation for his own ideas. *Freedom* was written in two languages, Latin and German. The Latin version was written for and sent to Pope Leo X, accompanied by an introductory letter, while the slightly different and shorter German version was sent to the mayor of Zwickau and was written for widespread dissemination throughout the German-speaking lands.

One of Luther's key doctrines, which he discussed in numerous publications, was justification by faith. The Bible, he argued, taught that humans had no ability to earn their own salvation but, through divine grace, were justified solely by faith. In *Freedom*, Luther built upon this fundamental idea to develop his doctrine of Christian liberty or freedom. By this he meant that, through God's gracious gift of faith, Christians required no acts or works to make them righteous or to save them. They were thus free of the chains of constant religious action or ritual required by the medieval church. They were also free of fear and death. This did not mean that Christians should not do good works or serve their neighbors, or that they were free to do whatever they liked. Luther argued that the very love they had for God, who had freed them, also bound them to act according to His will. "That is Christian freedom,"

Von der freyhait
ains Christen
menschen.
Martinus Luther.

M. D. XXI.

Frontispiece of *Von der Freyhait eins Christen menschen (On the Freedom of a Christian)* by Martin Luther (Augsburg, 1521). Courtesy of Bayerische Staatsbibliothek München.

Luther stated, "faith alone, which does not lead us to live in idleness or do wickedness, but instead means that we require no works to obtain piety and salvation."[1] This seemingly contradictory argument forms the heart of *Freedom*, and it was also a direct refutation of common church teachings, which argued that there was no salvation outside the embrace of the church and that Christians could aid in their own salvation. Christians were required to participate in the sacraments and to be members of the church and under its authority, and the relationship between worshipper and God was to be mediated by the priesthood. Luther rejected all this, and attempted to free Christians both from what he saw as the false authority of the priesthood and from what he viewed as a pointless struggle to satisfy God through works.

These were powerful concepts, and in Luther's introductory letter to Pope Leo X he argued that within *Freedom* lay "the entire sum of a Christian life." Whether one agrees with this assessment or not, there is no denying that *Freedom* was intensely popular. However, these concepts were also complex, and many ordinary people who read or learned of these ideas (and many did, due to the recent invention of the printing press) misunderstood Luther's meaning. Rather than seeing his idea of freedom in its intended religious or spiritual framework, some understood it more broadly, in a socioeconomic sense.[2] By 1524, such a more expansive understanding of political, social, and economic freedom had become the rallying cry of dissatisfied and frustrated peasants across the Holy Roman Empire, who revolted against authorities of all kinds in what has become known as the German Peasants' War (1524–1526). While these revolts were based more on local and historical conditions than on Luther's ideas, many blamed Luther for this bloody revolution and for the tens of thousands killed in it. Luther himself, horrified, published a scathing rebuke of the rebels titled *Against the Robbing and Murdering Hordes of Peasants*. Luther's *Freedom*, therefore, was the most influential of his three major 1520 publications, both among those who understood its intended message and those who did not.

---

1. Luther, *On the Freedom of a Christian*, §10.

2. For more on how Luther's idea of Christian freedom was interpreted, see Mark U. Edwards, "The Reception of Luther's Understanding of Freedom in the Early Modern Period," *Lutherjahrbuch* 62 (1995), 104–20.

Martin Luther, *An Open Letter to Pope Leo X*[1]

In a last-ditch attempt to heal the rift between Luther and the pope, in October 1519 the papal nuncio Karl von Miltitz convinced Luther to submit his case to the archbishop of Trier for mediation. This was unsuccessful, and in June 1520, at the urgings of Luther's enemy Johannes Eck and others at Rome, Luther was condemned in the papal bull Exsurge Domine. *Still hoping that some reconciliation might be possible, however, Miltitz then met with leaders of Luther's Augustinian order (Johann von Staupitz and his successor Wenzeslaus Linck) and convinced them to intervene with Luther. The resulting delegation, which arrived in Wittenberg in September, did indeed move Luther to write a letter in Latin to the pope and an accompanying explanation of his beliefs* (On the Freedom of a Christian). *Yet while Miltitz and the others had asked, and been assured by Luther, that the letter would be conciliatory, it was only polite on the surface—perhaps due to Luther's pique at Eck's recent arrival in the empire to disseminate the papal condemnation. Thinly veiled behind the compliments and concern in the letter was brutal criticism of Leo either as pathetically weak, deluded, and criminally blind to the sins of his court, or as complicit. And while Luther claimed in the letter to admire Leo's piety and personal character, he also denigrated the papal court in the strongest possible terms and violated usual protocol by addressing Leo as an equal—a clear insult but also a reiteration of Luther's argument that all men are spiritually equal. There is no record that Leo ever read the letter, though surely if he had, it would have done nothing to convince him of Luther's good will. The letter was read by many others, however, for it was published in Wittenberg separately from* Freedom *in German translation sometime before early November 1520. It would subsequently be published in numerous editions, both in Latin and German. The following translation is made from the German version of the letter.*

* * *

1. This translation is based on the German text given in Martin Luther, *D. Martin Luthers Werke: Kritische Gesamtausgabe*, vol. 7 (Weimar: H. Böhlau, 1897), 3–11.

To the Most Holy Father in God, Leo X, Pope in Rome, all blessedness in Jesus Christ, Our Lord. Amen.

Most Holy Father in God. The quarrel and dispute in which I have been involved for almost three years now[2] with a number of loathsome people of this time has forced me to look to you[3] from time to time, and to think of you. Indeed, because it is believed that you are the sole and principal cause of this dispute, I cannot help but think of you incessantly. For although I have been compelled by a number of your unchristian flatterers (who are roused against me without any cause) to appeal in my affair from your See and Curia[4] to a Christian, free council,[5] yet I have never alienated my feelings for you, so that with all my strength I have always wished the best for you and your Roman See, and have beseeched God with diligent, heartfelt prayers for this as much as I am able. It is true that I have indeed acted to scorn and to overcome those who have endeavored to intimidate me with the elevation and greatness of your name and power; but one thing has now arisen that I dare not scorn and that is the reason I am once again writing to you. And this is, namely, that I have become aware that I have been reviled and accused of evilness, for it is said I have not even spared your person.

However, I wish to profess freely and openly that as far as I am aware, whenever I have thought of your person, I have always said the

---

2. Since Luther began his campaign against the sale of indulgences in 1517.

3. Here Luther uses the familiar form of the German word for "you" and thus treats the pope as an equal, violating traditional hierarchical norms of the church and reinforcing his argument about the limits of papal authority.

4. The Papal See (from the Latin word for "seat") is the office or jurisdiction of the pope. The Roman Curia is the papal court, serving the pope as his bureaucracy and government.

5. The role of church councils was contested. Since the fourteenth century and in response to serious problems (such as the growth of heresy and, especially, a great schism caused by rival claimants to the papacy), the conciliar movement had claimed that the body of the church, as represented by church councils, had primacy over popes. This reform movement had enormous success in the early to mid-fifteenth century, but thereafter popes and their supporters vigorously challenged this attack on papal authority. By suggesting that a church council has the authority to overturn the decisions of the Papal Curia, Luther clearly suggests here his sympathy for the conciliar movement.

most honorable and best things about you. And had I ever done otherwise, I myself could in no way condone it, but would have to affirm the judgment of my critics with a full acknowledgment, and I would want nothing more than to repudiate my own recklessness and wickedness, and to recant my criminal words. I have called you a Daniel at Babylon[6] and everyone who reads can abundantly recognize how assiduously I have defended your innocence against the blasphemer Sylvester.[7]

Indeed, your reputation and the fame of your good life are known throughout the world, magnificently and greatly lauded by so many leading scholars that no one, however great he might be, could impugn it through any kind of trickery. I am not so foolish that I alone would attack him whom everyone praises, and it has always been (and I hope will also be from now on) my practice not to impugn even those whom everyone holds in ill repute. I take no pleasure in the sins of others, for I am well aware that I too have a beam in my eye,[8] and certainly cannot be the one to cast the first stone at the adulteress.[9]

I have indeed, though in general, sharply attacked several unchristian teachings and have been biting against my adversaries; but not on account of their evil lives, rather on account of their unchristian teachings and their defense of them. This is by no means something I regret, for I have resolved to persist in such zeal and severity, regardless of how others will construe this. And here I have the example of Christ, who out of severe zealousness also called his adversaries the offspring of vipers, hypocrites, blind, children of the devil;[10] and St. Paul called the sorcerer [Elymas] a child of the devil, who is full of wickedness

---

6. See Dan. 6:1–28, where Daniel's steadfast faith delivers him from the lions' den and impresses the Persian king Darius.

7. The Dominican theologian Sylvester Mazzolini, aka Sylvester Prieras (c. 1456–1523), who was a strong proponent of papal authority. In response to Luther's complaint about the selling of indulgences, Prieras argued that church teachings and actions, as overseen by the pope, were infallible, and anyone who disagreed was a heretic. Luther saw this as a blasphemous degradation of the authority of Scripture as well as an insult to the pope, who was in Luther's view a humble servant of the church, not its infallible master.

8. Matt. 7:3–5; Luke 6:41–42.

9. John 8:1–11.

10. Matt. 23:33, 13, 17; John 8:44.

and deceit;[11] and he scolded several false apostles as dogs, deceivers, and corrupters of God's word.[12] If tender, delicate ears had heard such things, they also surely would have said that no one was as biting and impatient as St. Paul. And who is more biting than the prophets? But in our time the crowd of pernicious sycophants has caused our ears to become so very delicate and tender, such that the moment we are not praised in all things, we cry out that our critics are being biting. And because we cannot otherwise ward off the truth, we absolve ourselves by means of the invented cause of snappishness, impatience, and immodesty. But what use is salt, if it does not bite sharply? What use is the blade of a sword, if it does not cut sharply? But the prophet says: "Cursed is the man who only follows God's commandments perfunctorily and is too sparing [in the use of his sword]."[13]

Therefore I beg you, Holy Father Leo, that you will accept this, my explanation, and truly consider me as one who would never undertake anything evil against your person; whose only intention is to wish and desire the very best for you; and who wants no quarrel or squabble with anyone on account of someone's evil life, but only on account of the truth of the divine word. In all other matters I will gladly yield to any man, yet I neither will nor may abandon or disavow the word of God. Anyone who expects otherwise from me, or who has otherwise understood my writings, errs and has not understood me properly.

It is however true: I have freshly impugned the Roman See, which they call the Roman Curia, and which neither you yourself, nor anyone else on earth, can fail to admit is more terrible and more shameful than even Sodom, Gomorrah, or Babylon were;[14] and so far as I can see, its wickedness can neither be aided nor helped. Everything there has become exceedingly desperate and abysmal. Thus I was chagrined that poor people throughout the world have been deceived and harmed in your name and under the pretext of the Roman Church; I have opposed this, and I will continue to oppose it so long as a

---

11. Acts 13:10.

12. Phil. 3:2; 2 Cor. 11:13, 2:17.

13. Jer. 48:10.

14. Cities described in the Bible as places of extraordinary and incorrigible sin and corruption.

Christian spirit lives within me. Not that I presume to achieve impossible things, or hope to rectify anything within the most dreadful Roman Sodom and Babylon, especially as so many furious sycophants resist me; instead I act because I perceive myself to be an indentured servant to all Christians: therefore it is granted to me to counsel and warn, so that at least fewer of them, and with fewer injuries, are ruined by the Roman destroyers.

For it is not hidden even from you how for many years now nothing but the ruin of bodies, souls, and goods, and all the most pernicious examples of every evil thing, have washed and burst forth from Rome throughout the world. All of this is openly and clearly known to everyone, such that the Roman Church, which previously was the most holy, has now become a thieves' den above all thieves' dens, a whorehouse above all whorehouses, a leader and kingdom of all sin, death, and damnation, such that it is hard to conceive what could add more wickedness there, even if the Antichrist himself were to come.

Meanwhile you, Holy Father Leo, sit like a lamb among the wolves,[15] and just like Daniel among the lions,[16] and with Ezekiel among scorpions.[17] What can you, one man, do against so many wild monsters? And even if you were to join with three or four learned pious cardinals, what are these among such a horde? You would surely perish from poison before you could begin to remedy matters.[18] The Roman See is finished; God's wrath has assailed it without end. It is an enemy of general councils, it will allow itself to be neither instructed nor reformed, and it is unable to hinder its own furious unchristian nature. Thus it fulfills what was said of its mother, the old Babylon: "We healed a great deal at Babylon, yet still she is not healed; let us forsake her."[19]

It should have been your and the cardinals' work to resist this misery, but the sickness mocks the remedy; horse and wagon do not yield

---

15. Matt. 10:16.
16. Dan. 6:16.
17. Ezek. 2:6.
18. Leo survived just such a plot to poison him by a group of cardinals in summer 1517; a clear sign of the vicious infighting and corruption among the leaders of the church.
19. Jer. 51:9.

to the wagoner. This is the reason why I have always been sorry that you, pious Leo, have become pope in this time, for you are surely worthy of being pope in better times. The Roman See is unworthy of you and those like you; the evil spirit [Satan] should instead be pope, for he certainly rules in that Babylon more than you do.

O would God that you, freed of this honor (as those who are your most pernicious enemies call it), might instead maintain yourself through a benefice[20] or your paternal inheritance! In truth, no one but Judas Iscariot[21] and his kind, whom God has cast out, should justly be dignified with such an honor.[22] Tell me, then, how are you of any use to the papacy? For the more terrible and desperate it is, the more and the more intensely your power and title are misused to harm the people in their goods and souls, to increase sin and shame, and to stifle faith and truth. O you most unfortunate Leo, for you sit on the most dangerous seat. Verily, I tell you the truth; for I wish you well.

If St. Bernard lamented for his Pope Eugenius[23]—who, although the Roman See was also extremely terrible at that time, still ruled in good hope of improvement—how much more should we then lament for you, since in these three hundred years wickedness and ruin have so irresistibly gained the upper hand! Is it not true that there is nothing under the wide heavens that is more terrible, more poisonous, and more hateful than the Roman Curia? It far surpasses the immorality of the Turks, for while it is true that Rome previously was a gate of heaven, now it is an unlocked mouth of hell and alas, due to the wrath of God, such a mouth as no one can shut. And now we have no

---

20. A benefice was a grant or allotment, usually the lifetime right to collect certain ecclesiastical revenues or taxes, given to priests or higher churchmen for their financial support. Technically, benefices imposed some sort of religious duties on the holder, though these were easily ignored.

21. Judas Iscariot was one of the Twelve Apostles, infamous for his betrayal of Jesus Christ.

22. John 17:12.

23. The French abbot St. Bernard of Clairvaux (1090–1153) sent to Pope Eugenius III (r. 1145–1153) his book *On Consideration*, in which he warned Eugenius about the dangers of his office and suggested that reform of the church began with the piety of the pope himself.

remaining option but to warn and preserve some few so that they are not devoured by this Roman mouth.

You see, my Lord Father, this is the cause and the impetus for why I have struck so hard against this pestilential See. In fact, so far was I from intending to rage against your person, that I had even hoped I might earn your blessing and thanks, and, since I so vigorously and sharply attacked your prison, indeed your hell, be recognized as dealing in your best interests. For I think that everything that reasonable, educated men can accomplish against the ruinous disorders of your unchristian Curia would be good and blessed for you and many others. In truth, all who only do harm and evil to such a Curia are doing something that you should; all who put this Curia to the greatest shame are honoring Christ. In short, all good Christians are bad Romans.

And, may I add, it would never have come into my heart to have grumbled against the Roman Curia or to have contended something against it; but when I saw that it was not to be helped, that costs and effort were wasted, then I scorned it, sent it a farewell letter, and said: "Goodbye, dear Rome; whatever stinks, let it stink from now on, and whatever is unclean, let it remain unclean forever and ever."[24] I thus adjourned to the quiet, calm study of the Holy Scriptures, so that I might be helpful to those with whom I lived. When this proved fruitful, the Evil Spirit opened his eyes and became aware of it. Swiftly he aroused in his servant Johannes Eck,[25] a special enemy of Christ and the truth, a nonsensical ambition, and suggested to him that he drag me unexpectedly into a disputation and seize upon a little word spoken about the papacy that I had more or less let slip out.[26] Then this great vainglorious hero [Eck], frothing and snorting, made out as if he had already imprisoned me; he professed that he would risk and undertake

---

24. Rev. 22:11.

25. Johannes Eck (1486–1543), a leading theologian and professor at Ingolstadt, and Martin Luther's most vociferous opponent.

26. In July 1519, Eck met Luther at Leipzig for a public theological disputation or debate over such issues as free will, divine grace, and papal authority. Here Eck forced Luther to admit his agreement with some of the positions of the Bohemian heretic Jan Hus and to deny the authority of the papacy and councils in matters of faith.

everything for the honor of God and the glory of the Holy Roman Church. He puffed himself up and presumed your authority, which he hoped to use not for the papacy, but to have himself called the foremost theologian in the world—something he certainly expected. He imagined that it would be no small benefit for him to be victorious over Doctor Luther. But when that went awry, the sophist[27] became nonsensical; for he now felt as if it were his fault alone that the shame and disgrace of the Roman See had been revealed to me.

Allow me now, Holy Father, to argue my case to you this once, and to indict your true enemies. It is surely known to you how Cardinal St. Sisto,[28] your legate, dealt with me at Augsburg; in truth, presumptuously and unjustly, indeed also unfaithfully, although for your sake I placed my entire case in his hands so that he could command peace. I wanted an end to the matter and would have held my peace as long as my adversaries were also quiet, something he easily could have achieved with one word. Yet the thrill of worldly fame itched at him so much that he scorned my proposition, dared to vindicate my adversaries, to give them an even longer bridle, and to command that I recant, although he had no orders to do so. Thus it happened that through his willful recklessness the matter, which was at the time in a good state, became much worse. Therefore, what then followed is not my fault but this same cardinal's, who would not allow me to be silent, as I so earnestly requested. What more should I have done?

Afterwards Karl von Miltitz,[29] also a nuncio of Your Holiness, arrived, traveled here and there with great effort, and exercised every diligence to bring the matter once again to that good state from which the cardinal had arrogantly and recklessly expelled it. Finally, through the help of His Most Serene and Distinguished Highness, Elector

---

27. The Sophists were ancient Greek philosophers and teachers known for their rhetorical skills. Later the term came to refer to anyone who skillfully and ingeniously argued points without reference to their actual truth or morality.

28. Cardinal St. Sisto (1469–1534), also known as Thomas Cajetan, was a leading theologian and the head of the Dominican Order. He met Luther at Augsburg in October 1518 to discuss Luther's arguments against indulgences—a meeting that did not end well.

29. Karl von Miltitz (1490–1529), a papal nuncio or ambassador.

Frederick, duke of Saxony,[30] he arranged to speak with me several times.[31] Here, out of respect for your name, I once again resigned myself to be silent, and agreed to have the matter heard and decided by the archbishop of Trier or the bishop of Naumburg; which was then arranged and ordered. But while things were quite hopeful and peaceful, your greatest true enemy, Johannes Eck, now broke in with his above-mentioned disputation at Leipzig that he had undertaken against Dr. Karlstadt,[32] and with his fickle words found a little ruse related to the papacy and suddenly turned upon me with all his forces and might, so that the intended peace proposal was entirely destroyed.

Meanwhile Karl [von Miltitz] was waiting. The disputation went forward, judges were chosen, but nothing was achieved.[33] This did not surprise me, for Eck had so embittered, confused, and shattered matters with his lies, open letters, and secret practices, that regardless of which side would have won the judgment, undoubtedly a greater fire would have been lit, for he sought fame, not the truth. Thus I have always done what was enjoined on me, and have omitted nothing that I was supposed to do. I do acknowledge that no small part of the unchristian nature of Rome has come to light through this case. But the blame for this is not mine, but Eck's, for he undertook a matter for which he was not man enough, and through his ambition the afflictions of Rome have been displayed throughout the world, to its shame.

This man, Holy Father Leo, is the enemy of you and of the Roman See. From his example everyone may learn that there is no more damaging enemy than a sycophant. What has he wrought with his flattery but misfortune like that no king could have brought about? The Roman Curia's name now stinks wickedly throughout the world, the

---

30. Elector Frederick III of Saxony (1463–1525) was one of the leading princes of the empire. He founded and sponsored the University of Wittenberg, where Martin Luther taught.

31. These conferences occurred at Altenburg in January 1519, in Liebenwerda in October 1519, and in Lichtenberg in October 1520.

32. The Leipzig debate (mentioned above) began as a disputation between Eck and Andreas Bodenstein von Karlstadt (c. 1482–1541), Luther's friend and colleague, before Luther himself was drawn in.

33. The judges failed to offer a verdict in the debate.

papal ban is feeble, and Roman ignorance has an evil repute. Yet no one would have heard any of this if Eck had not disturbed my and Karl's peace proposal. This is also something he himself now perceives, and he is, though too late and in vain, indignant about the little books I have published. He should have thought of that before, when he whin- nied for fame like a spirited, lustful horse and sought nothing but his own benefit, to your great disadvantage. He thought, the vain man, that I would fear your name and so give way to him and be silent (for I think he did not presume to have the necessary skill and cleverness). Now that he sees that I am yet encouraged and will be heard further, he feels a tardy regret for his recklessness and becomes aware (if he indeed does) that there is One in heaven who resists the arrogant and humbles presumptuous spirits.[34]

Since nothing was achieved through the disputation but greater dishonor for the Roman See, Karl Miltitz came to the fathers of my order[35] and sought advice on how to reconcile and quiet the matter, which was then in the most ruinous and dangerous state. Then several of their leaders were sent to me, for it was not supposed that anything could be accomplished against me through force. They requested that I honor your person, Holy Father, and write a humble letter to explain both your and my innocence [in this affair], thinking that the mat- ter was not yet desperate and lost into the abyss, provided that Holy Father Leo, out of his inherent and most illustrious goodness, would take it in hand. Because I have always offered and desired peace so that I might attend to calmer and better studies, I considered this delega- tion to be pleasing and joyous. I received them with thanks and most willingly allowed myself to be directed. Indeed, I recognized this as a special mercy, if only it might happen as we hoped. For the only reason I so boldly bestirred myself and made noise with my words and writ- ings was to overwhelm and quiet them [my opponents], for I saw well that they were far from my equals.

Therefore I now come, Holy Father Leo, and, prostrate at your feet, beg you to take this matter in hand as far as possible and to rein in the

---

34. 1 Pet. 5:5; James 4:6.
35. The monastic Order of St. Augustine.

sycophants, who are the enemies of peace and yet profess peace. But for me to recant my teachings is impossible, and no one should attempt to force this unless he wishes to drive the matter into an even greater confusion. Furthermore, I will not endure rules for, or limits to, my interpretation of the Scriptures; for the word of God, which teaches every freedom, should not and must not be imprisoned.[36] If these two points are adhered to, then there is nothing else that could be imposed upon me that I would not most willingly do and endure. I am the enemy of strife and do not wish to incite or provoke anyone; yet I also do not wish to be provoked. Should I be provoked, however, I shall, if God wills, be neither speechless nor without my quill. With simple, easy words, Your Holiness can claim jurisdiction over all of this strife and obliterate it, and instead command silence and peace—something I have always been most eager to hear.

Therefore, my Holy Father, you should not listen to the sweet sirens who say that you are not a mere man, but are mingled with God, who can command and require all things. Things will not happen in this way, and you will not be able to make them happen. You are a servant of all the servants of God,[37] and in a more dangerous and more wretched situation than any man on earth. Do not let yourself be deceived by those who lie and pretend you are a lord of the world; who will allow no one to be Christian unless he is subject to you; and who babble that you have authority over heaven, hell, and purgatory. They are your enemies and seek to ruin your soul. As Isaiah said: "My dear people, those who praise and exalt you, deceive you."[38] All err who say that you are above a council and general Christendom. They err who give you alone the power to interpret Scripture. They, all of them, seek nothing more than how they might, under your name, strengthen their unchristian enterprises within Christendom—just as the Evil Spirit has, alas, done through many of your predecessors. In short, believe no one who exalts you, but only those who humble you. That is God's

---

36. 2 Tim. 2:9.

37. Servant of the servants of God (*Servus Servorum Dei* in Latin) was one of the titles of the pope. See also Matt. 20:25–27.

38. Isa. 3:12.

judgment, as it is written: "He has put down the mighty from their seats, and exalted the lowly."[39]

See how different Christ is from His vicars[40] if, in fact, they do all wish to be His vicars. In truth, I fear they are all too truly His vicars, for a vicar is only a vicar in the absence of his master. If then a pope rules in the absence of Christ and without Him living within his heart, is he then not all too truly Christ's vicar? What then can such a flock be but a gathering without Christ? What then can such a pope be but an Antichrist and idol? How much better did the apostles act, who merely called themselves (and allowed themselves to be called) servants of the Christ within them, not vicars of an absent one![41]

Perhaps I am being presumptuous in thinking to teach such a great dignitary, indeed one by whom everyone should be taught and, as several of your poisonous sycophants boast, from whom all the thrones of kings and judges receive their judgments. But here I am following St. Bernard in his book to Pope Eugenius,[42] which all popes should justly know by heart. I do it not with the intention of teaching you, but out of the pure faithful concern and duty that justly require every man to concern himself with the affairs of his neighbors, even if they seem secure, and do not allow us to consider either status or lack of status, but instead to focus assiduously on our neighbors' danger or advantage. For I well know how Your Holiness is tossed here and there at Rome, as if on the roughest sea, with innumerable hazards storming from all sides, and how you live and work in such misery that you surely need the help of even the most humble Christian. Thus I have not considered it to be ill conceived to forget your majesty until

---

39. Luke 1:52.

40. The German word Luther uses here is *Statthalter*, which literally means "placeholder" and indicates a person who commands or rules in the place of an absent ruler as his governor, vice-regent, lieutenant, or deputy. Within the Catholic Church, the title "vicar" (from the Latin *vicarious*, meaning deputy or lieutenant) is used similarly, and is given to representatives or deputies of church officials such as popes or bishops. The special title "vicar of Christ" (*Vicarius Christi*) is held by the pope.

41. Phil. 1:1.

42. See note 23 above.

I can satisfy the duty of brotherly love. I do not wish to flatter you in so serious and dangerous a matter in which, though many will not understand me, I am your friend and more than subservient to you; he who understands will indeed see this.

In conclusion, so that I do not come empty-handed before Your Holiness, I send with my good wishes a little book, dedicated to you,[43] to further peace and with the good hope that Your Holiness may sense from it the kind of activities I wish to pursue—and might do so fruitfully if only your unchristian flatterers would allow it. If one considers the paper, it is but a little book; but if one understands the meaning, one sees that the entire sum of a Christian life is contained within. I am poor and have nothing else with which I might render my services, but you need nothing but spiritual possessions to better you. With this I commend myself to Your Holiness, whom Jesus Christ preserves forever, Amen.

At Wittenberg, 6 September 1520[44]

---

43. *On the Freedom of a Christian.*

44. The letter was actually written over a month later, but backdated to make it appear as if Luther were not writing in response to *Exsurge Domine.*

Martin Luther, *On the Freedom of a Christian*[1]

At the heart of Freedom *are the words of Paul: "I am free in all things and have made myself a servant of everyone." (1 Cor. 9:19). This is a contradiction that Luther explores carefully and thoroughly in the thirty points, or theses, below.* Freedom *was written in Latin for the pope, and then Luther composed a slightly shorter German version that he forwarded to the mayor of the town of Zwickau, in Thuringia. Both versions were quickly published, with the German seeing over twenty editions by mid-century, the Latin at least eight. The following is a translation of the German version.*

* * *

To the prudent and wise Mister Hieronymus Mühlpfordt,[2] mayor of Zwickau, my especially kind friend and patron; I, Dr. Martin Luther, Augustinian, offer my willing service and best wishes.

Prudent, wise gentleman and kind friend:

Your laudable city preacher, the worthy Master Johannes Egran,[3] has highly commended you to me for the love and passion that you have for the Holy Scripture, which you also diligently profess and do not cease to praise before men. For this reason he desired to acquaint me with you, and I was quite easily, willingly, and happily persuaded of this, for it is a special joy for me to hear of a place where divine truth is beloved, since unfortunately so many, and especially those who

---

1. This translation is based on the German text given in Martin Luther, *D. Martin Luthers Werke. Kritische Gesamtausgabe*, vol. 7 (Weimar: H. Böhlau, 1897), 20–38.

2. Hermann Mühlpfordt the Elder (1486–1534). Here Luther accidentally calls him by the wrong name, Hieronymus (or Jerome).

3. Johannes Egranus (c. 1480–1535), a preacher in Zwickau since 1516. Soon after the publication of *Freedom*, he and Luther had a falling out over Egranus' relationship with the radical reformer Thomas Müntzer.

boast of their titles, struggle against it with all their power and guile. Yet it must be that Christ, who is set as a stumbling block and a sign that must be spoken against, will cause many to stumble, fall, and arise again.[4] Therefore, in order to begin our acquaintanceship and friendship, I wanted to dedicate to you this small treatise and sermon in German—which I have dedicated to the pope in Latin—so that the basis of my teaching and writing on the papacy is, I hope, shown to be one that no one can condemn. I hereby commend myself to you, and all of us to divine grace. Amen. At Wittenberg, 1520.

* * *

Introduction[5]

Jesus

1. So that we might thoroughly discern what a Christian is and the nature of the freedom that Christ obtained for and gave to him, about which St. Paul has written so much, I shall posit these two conclusions:

A Christian is a free lord of all things and is subject to no one.

A Christian is a dutiful servant in all things and is subject to everyone.

These two conclusions are clear from St. Paul, in 1 Corinthians 9: "I am free in all things and have made myself a servant of everyone."[6] Likewise in Romans 13: "You shall owe no one anything, except that you love one another."[7] Yet love is dutiful and subject to that which is

---

4. See 1 Cor. 1:22–23; Isa. 8:14–15; Luke 2:34.

5. This and all subsequent section headers were not in Luther's original; I add them here for clarity.

6. 1 Cor. 9:19. Here Luther accidentally cited 1 Cor. 12, an error corrected in the Weimar edition and correctly given by Luther in the Latin version. Note that throughout this document I give literal translations of Luther's German-language Bible quotes, rather than using any specific English-language version of the Bible.

7. Rom. 13:8.

loved. And so in reference to Christ, in Galatians 4: "God sent forth His Son, born of a woman and made subject to the law."[8]

2. To resolve these two contradictory statements on freedom and servitude, we shall consider that every Christian has a double nature: a spiritual and a physical. In regard to the soul, he is called a spiritual, new, internal man;[9] in regard to flesh and blood, he is called a physical, old, and external man. And it is because of these differences that, as I have just said, he is mentioned in the Scriptures both in terms of freedom and servitude, one directly contrary to another.

The Internal Man

3. When we consider the interior, spiritual man in order to see what would be necessary for him to be, and to be called, a pious,[10] free Christian, it becomes clear that no external thing, of whatever name, can make him either free or pious; for his piety and freedom, or, on the other hand, his wickedness and imprisonment, are neither physical nor external. How does it help the soul if the body is unbound, fresh, and healthy, and eats, drinks, and lives however it likes? On the other hand, how does it damage the soul if the body is imprisoned, sick, and feeble, and hungers, thirsts, and suffers against its wishes? None of

---

8. Gal. 4:4.

9. Luther uses the masculine form of the word *mensch*, which in his time could mean either "man" (most commonly) or "person." I have translated *mensch* as "man" throughout this document, both as it seems closer to his intent, and as it more precisely reflects common sixteenth-century understandings of men as the standard or model of humanity. That is not at all to say that Luther meant to exclude women from his understanding of Christian liberty, as he often argued that women and men were spiritually equal, though unequal in all other ways. For this reason, wherever Luther uses the phrase *Christen Mensch* I have translated this as simply "Christian," while keeping the male gender of associated pronouns.

10. The word Luther uses here is *frum* (i.e., *fromm*), by which he means not only pious, religious, or upright, but also justified and righteous. However, as elsewhere in the text he specifically uses other German words for the latter two terms, I have maintained the translation of "pious" for all uses of *frum* throughout this document.

these things reach the soul, either to free or imprison her,[11] or to make her pious or evil.

4. Thus it is no help for the soul if the body puts on holy garments,[12] as do the priests and clergy; nor if the body is in churches and holy places; nor if it is occupied with holy matters; nor if it physically prays, fasts, goes on a pilgrimage, and does every good work that might only ever happen through and in the body.[13] It must then be something entirely different that brings and bestows piety and freedom to the soul. For an evil man, a hypocrite and fraud, may also possess or practice all of these above-mentioned objects, works, and manners. In this way, furthermore, people become nothing more than pure hypocrites. On the other hand, it does not damage the soul if the body wears unholy garments, is in unholy places, eats, drinks, does not go on a pilgrimage, and omits all the works that the above-mentioned hypocrite performs.

5. There is nothing, either in heaven or on earth, through which the soul can live and be pious, free, and Christian, besides the holy gospel, the word of God preached by Christ. As He Himself says in John 11: "I am the life and the resurrection, whoever believes in Me, lives forever."[14] Also John 14: "I am the way, the truth, and the life."[15] Likewise in Matthew 4: "Man does not live on bread alone, but on every word that comes from the mouth of God."[16] So we can now be certain that the soul can dispense with everything but the word of God, and without the word of God nothing can help her. Where she has the word, however, she requires nothing more; rather, in the word she has enough food, joy, peace, light, skill, righteousness, truth, wisdom, freedom, and everything good in great abundance. Thus we read in

---

11. I have used the feminine pronoun here, both as in German "the soul" is a feminine noun and as Luther conceives of the soul as a passive vessel for God's grace, much as he saw a woman as passive in relationship to a man.

12. Cf. Exod. 28:2, 28:4, etc.

13. Note that Luther uses the word "work" to encompass both outwardly physical actions and what we might consider purely mental or intellectual actions.

14. John 11:25, 11:26.

15. John 14:6.

16. Matt. 4:4.

the Psalms, especially in Psalm 118, that the prophet cries out for nothing but the word of God.[17] And in the Scriptures it is deemed the greatest plague and wrath of God when He withdraws His word from mankind. On the other hand, there is no greater grace than when He sends out His word, as it states in Psalm 106: "He sent out His word, whereby He might help them."[18] And Christ came for no other purpose than to preach the word of God. Also all apostles, bishops, priests, and the entire clergy were called and instituted solely for the sake of the word; although, unfortunately, this is not how things work now.

6. But you may ask: "What, then, is the word that gives such great grace, and how shall I use it?" Answer: It is nothing other than the preaching of Christ as contained in the gospel, which should be, and indeed is, presented so that you hear your God speak to you, explaining how all of your life and works are nothing to God, but must, along with all that is within you, eternally perish. If you truly believe this, that you are guilty, then you must despair of yourself and profess the truth of the words of Hosea: "O Israel, in you there is nothing but your own destruction; but in Me alone is your help."[19] However, so that you might come out of yourself and leave yourself, that is, avoid your destruction, He sets before you His beloved Son Jesus Christ, and through His living, comforting word tells you: You should surrender yourself to Him with firm faith and trust in Him anew. Then, for the sake of this faith, all your sins shall be forgiven, your destruction entirely overcome, and you shall be righteous,

---

17. Ps. 119:145–47. This is one of a number of citations Luther gives according to a numbering of the Psalms as given in the Latin Vulgate, which was the most common translation of the Bible used in the Middle Ages (and which had the same enumeration of the Psalms as the older Greek Septuagint). However, Luther later used the Hebrew-language Masoretic Text, which has a slightly different numbering system, as the basis of his 1534 German translation of the Old Testament. The Masoretic Text also became the standard basis for other Protestant bibles.

18. Ps. 107:20. Here Luther mistakenly wrote "Psalm 104," though this was corrected to "Psalm 106" in the Weimar edition (again, the numbering as given in the Vulgate).

19. Hos. 13:9.

truthful, tranquil, pious, and shall have fulfilled all commandments, free of all things. As St. Paul says in Romans 1: "A justified Christian lives by his faith alone."[20] And in Romans 10: "Christ is the end and the fulfillment of all commandments for those who believe in Him."[21]

7. Thus the only work and exercise of all Christians should rightly be that they establish the word and Christ within themselves, continuously exercising and strengthening such a faith. For no other work can make a Christian. As Christ, in John 6, told the Jews when they asked Him what kind of works they should do that would be divine and Christian works; He said: "The only divine work is that you believe in the One whom God has sent"[22] and whom God the Father has alone ordained for this purpose. Therefore a proper faith in Christ is indeed wealth in great abundance, for He brings with Him all beatitude[23] and takes away all wretchedness. As in Mark, the last chapter: "He who believes and is baptized shall be saved. He who does not believe shall be damned."[24] Thus the prophet Isaiah, in chapter 10, considered the wealth of this same faith and said: "God will make a brief accounting on the earth, and the brief accounting will, like a deluge, overflow with righteousness."[25] That is, faith, which is in short the fulfilling of all commandments, will abundantly justify all those who have it, such that they require nothing more to be righteous and pious. Thus St. Paul said in Romans 10: "If one believes from his heart, he is made righteous and pious."[26]

8. But how does it happen that faith alone can make one pious and, without any works, give such greatly abundant wealth, when so many

---

20. Rom. 1:17. Here Luther, in order to emphasize his larger point, adds the word "alone" to Paul's statement.

21. Rom. 10:4.

22. John 6:28–6:29.

23. Supreme blessedness or happiness.

24. Mark 16:16.

25. Cf. Isa. 10:22–25.

26. Rom. 10:10.

laws, commandments, works, estates,[27] and ways are prescribed for us in the Scriptures? Here one should diligently note and indeed earnestly remember that faith alone, without any works, makes one pious, free, and saved, as we will hear more about later. And one should know that the entire Holy Scripture is divided into two types of words, that is, God's commandment or law, and the promise or assurance. The commandments teach us and prescribe for us various good works, but yet they are not followed. They show the way, but do not help; they teach what one should do, but give no strength to do so. Therefore they are only designated so that man might see within them his own incapacity for good and learn to despair of himself. And therefore they are also called the old testament, and all belong in the Old Testament.[28] As the commandment: "You shall not have evil desire"[29] shows that we are, all of us, sinners, and no man is able to be without evil desires, whatever he might do. From this he learns to give up hope in himself and to seek help elsewhere in order to be without evil desire; and so the commandment is fulfilled through another, for he does not have the capacity within himself. Thus all other commandments are also impossible for us.

9. Now when a man has learned of and perceived his own incapacity from the commandments, he will be fearful about how to satisfy the commandments; for the commandments must be fulfilled, or he will be damned. Thus he is rightly humbled and reduced to nothing in his own eyes, and finds nothing within himself that might make him pious. But then the other word, the divine promise or assurance, appears and says: If you will fulfill all commandments and be free of all of your wicked desires and sin (as the commandments oblige and

---

27. "Estates" is a term meaning social position or rank. Elsewhere in his writings Luther adopted the common medieval idea that all people (even unbelievers) naturally and by God's will belong within one (or more) of the three major walks of life or estates (*Stände*), including the church, the household or economic life, and civil government or political life. He then distinguishes this from vocations or callings, to which believing Christians are drawn by the Holy Spirit.

28. Here Luther is using the phrase "old testament" not, as is traditionally used by Christians, to mean the Hebrew Scriptures (i.e., the Old Testament), but instead as a way of describing any portion of the Bible that contains the commandments or laws of God.

29. I.e., "you shall not covet." Exod. 20:17.

require), then behold, believe in Christ, in whom, I assure you, is all grace, righteousness, peace, and freedom. Believe, and you will have this; do not believe, and you will not have this. For what is impossible for you to achieve through all the works of the commandments—which are necessarily numerous, and yet useless—will be easy and quick for you through faith. For I have, in short, placed everything onto faith; he who has it shall have everything and be saved; he who does not have it shall have nothing.[30] Thus the assurances of God give what the commandments require, and accomplish what the commandments decree. In this way everything, both commandment and fulfillment, is God's own; He alone decrees and He alone fulfills. Therefore the assurances of God are words of the new testament, and also belong in the New Testament.[31]

10. Now these, and all other words of God, are holy, truthful, righteous, peaceful, free, and full of all goodness. Therefore whoever adheres to them with a proper faith will find his soul so utterly united with Him that all the virtues of the word will also become intrinsic to his soul. And thus, through faith, the soul by God's word becomes holy, righteous, truthful, peaceful, free, and full of all goodness; a true child of God, as it says in John 1: "He has given to all those who believe in His name, that they might become children of God."[32]

From this it is readily apparent why faith is capable of so much, and why good works cannot be its equal. For good works do not depend on the divine word, as faith does, nor can they reside within the soul, since only the word and faith reign within the soul. As is the nature of the word, so too will be the nature of the soul,[33] just as iron glows red like fire from a union with fire. Thus we see that in faith a Christian

---

30. Mark 16:16: "The one who believes and is baptized will be saved; but the one who does not believe will be condemned."

31. As above with his use of "old testament," here Luther is using "new testament" not with the traditional understanding of the Christian Scriptures (i.e., the New Testament), but instead all those portions of the Bible that contain God's promises or covenants.

32. John 1:12.

33. In other words, the word imparts its qualities to the soul or the soul takes its nature from the word.

has enough, and no works are required to make him pious; and if he requires no further works, then he is certainly released from all commandments and laws; if he is released, then he is certainly free. That is Christian freedom: faith alone, which does not lead us to live in idleness or do wickedness, but instead means that we require no works to obtain piety and salvation. Later on we shall speak further on this matter.

11. In addition, when it comes to faith, it happens that when one believes in another man, he does so because he considers him to be a pious, truthful man, which is the greatest honor that one person can give another; on the contrary, it is the greatest disgrace if he considers him to be loose, mendacious, and frivolous. Thus also, if the soul firmly believes in God's word, then she deems Him truthful, pious, and righteous; thereby she gives Him the very greatest honor that she can give Him, for she then recognizes that He is correct, accepts His justice, honors His name, and allows Him to do with her as He will, for she does not doubt that He is pious and truthful in all of His words. On the other hand, one can offer God no greater dishonor than not to believe Him, so that the soul deems Him incapable, mendacious, and frivolous, and, as much as she can, denies Him with such unbelief and raises her own mind up as an idol in her heart, contrary to God, as if she would know better than He. When, however, God sees that the soul considers Him truthful and thus honors Him through her faith, then He honors her in turn, and also deems her pious and truthful, and through such faith she also becomes pious and truthful. For to consider God as truth and piety is right and true, and makes a man right and truthful. Therefore it is true and right that God be considered truth. Yet this is not done by those who do not believe, even though they strive to perform many good works.

12. Not only does faith give so much that the soul, like the divine word, becomes full of every grace, free, and saved; but the soul also unites with Christ like a bride with her bridegroom. From this marriage it follows, as St. Paul says, that Christ and the soul become one body,[34] so that both also hold everything in common, including both fortune

---

34. Eph. 5:30: "Because we are members of His body, of His flesh, and of His bones."

and misfortune; thus whatever Christ has, these are the believing soul's own; whatever the soul has, becomes Christ's own. As Christ has all goodness and blessedness,[35] these are the soul's own. As the soul has all vice and sin within herself, these become Christ's own. Here now arises the happy exchange and struggle. Because Christ is God and man, who has never sinned, and His piety is invincible, eternal, and omnipotent, He thus takes on the sin of the believing soul through her wedding ring, which is faith, and acts just as if He had done the sin Himself; thus sins are necessarily swallowed up and drowned in Him. For His invincible righteousness is too strong for all sins, and thus the soul is unfettered and freed of all her sins purely through her dowry, that is, for the sake of faith, and she is dowered with the eternal righteousness of her bridegroom, Christ. Now is this not a happy wedding celebration, when the rich, noble, pious bridegroom Christ takes the poor, despised, evil whore in marriage, absolves her of all wickedness, and adorns her with all goodness? For it is not possible for her sins to damn her, for they are now laid upon Christ and are swallowed up in Him; thus she has in her bridegroom such a rich righteousness that she can henceforth resist all sins, even if they were already laid upon her. Paul speaks about this in 1 Corinthians 15: "Praise and thank God, who has given us such a victory in Jesus Christ, in whom death and sin are swallowed up."[36]

13. Here, then, you see why so much is rightly attributed to faith; it fulfills all commandments and makes one pious without all other works. For you see here that by itself it fulfills the first commandment, which commands: "You shall honor one God."[37] Now if you were made purely of good works down to your toes, yet you would still not be pious nor do God any honor, and would thus not be fulfilling the very first commandment. For God is not honored unless truth and everything good, which are truly His, are attributed to Him. But no good works can accomplish this, rather the faith of the heart alone. Therefore faith alone is the righteousness of mankind and the fulfillment of

---

35. *Seligkeit*. Elsewhere I have translated this as "salvation," but the word can mean both.

36. 1 Cor. 15:57.

37. Deut. 5:7 and Exod. 20:3: "You shall have no other gods before Me."

all commandments. For whoever fulfills the first and principal commandment also fulfills all other commandments with certainty and ease. Works, however, are dead things, which can neither honor nor praise God, no matter how they are done or even if they are intended to honor and praise God. But here we do not seek which works are to be done, but rather the builder and master workman who honors God and does the works. This is no other than the faith of the heart, which is the principal and whole essence of piety. Therefore it is a dangerous and sinister thing to say, if one teaches that God's commandments are fulfilled through works, as the fulfillment must occur through faith before all works, and works then follow after the fulfillment, as we shall hear.

14. In order to see further what we have in Christ and how great a good proper faith is, one should know that before and in the Old Testament, God set aside and reserved for Himself all firstborn males of men and beasts;[38] and the firstborn was precious and had two great advantages over all other children, namely sovereignty and priestly offices, or kingship and priesthood,[39] such that on earth the firstborn boy child was a lord over all his brothers and a priest or pope before God. This figure symbolizes Jesus Christ, who was in actuality the self-same firstborn male of God the Father by the Virgin Mary. Therefore He is a king and priest, though spiritually, for His kingdom is neither earthly nor of earthly possessions, but of spiritual possessions such as truth, wisdom, peace, joy, salvation, etc. Temporal possessions are not thereby excluded, however, for all things in heaven, on earth, and in hell are subject to Him, although one does not see Him, that is, He rules spiritually, invisibly.

His priesthood thus does not consist in external gestures and garments, as we see among men, rather it consists in the spirit and so is invisible, such that He stands unceasingly before God's eyes and sacrifices Himself on behalf of His own, and does everything that a pious priest should do. He intercedes for us, as St. Paul says

---

38. Exod. 13:2: "Consecrate to Me all the firstborn; whatever is the first to open the womb among the Israelites, of human beings and animals, is Mine."
39. Gen. 49:3. Here Jacob speaks to his sons: "Reuben, you are my firstborn, my might and the first fruits of my vigor, excelling in rank and excelling in power."

in Romans 8;[40] similarly, He teaches us internally in our hearts. These are the two actual and proper offices of a priest, for external, human, temporal priests also intercede and teach.

15. Now since Christ was the firstborn, with its honor and worth, He then shares this with all of His Christians, so that, through faith, they must also all become kings and priests with Christ. As St. Paul says in 1 Peter 2: "You are a priestly kingdom and a kingly priesthood."[41] And the result is that a Christian, through faith, is elevated so high over all things that he becomes a spiritual lord of everything, for nothing can damage his salvation. Yes, all things must be subject to him and help him to salvation. As St. Paul teaches in Romans 8: "All things must help for the good of the predestined,"[42] whether these be life, death, sin, piety, good and evil, or whatever else one can name. Likewise, in 1 Corinthians 3, "all things are yours, whether life or death, past or future, etc."[43] Not that we are physically powerful over all things, to possess or to use them as other men on earth do, for we must physically die and no one may escape death. So too must we be governed by many other things, as were Christ and His saints. For this is a spiritual sovereignty, which rules through suppression of the body; that is, I can improve in my soul without the aid of any object, and even death and suffering must serve me and be useful toward my salvation. This is indeed a high, eminent dignity and a truly omnipotent sovereignty, a spiritual kingdom where nothing is so good or so evil that it must not serve to my good, so long as I believe; and yet nothing is required, for my faith is sufficient for me. Behold then what a precious freedom and power Christians possess!

16. In addition, we are priests, which is far more than being a king, because the priesthood makes us worthy to stand before God and intercede for others. For the right to stand before God's eyes and intercede is granted to none but priests. Therefore Christ has obtained for us that we might spiritually stand and intercede for another, like

---

40. Rom. 8:34.
41. 1 Pet. 2:9.
42. Rom. 8:28.
43. 1 Cor. 3:21–23.

a priest physically stands and intercedes for the people. However, he who does not believe in Christ has nothing that serves to his good; he is a servant in all things and must be vexed by all things. In addition, his prayers are not pleasing and do not come before God's eyes. Who now can conceive of the honor and elevation of a Christian? Through his kingdom he is powerful in all things, through his priesthood he is powerful before God, for God does what he asks and wishes, as is written in the Book of Psalms: "God fulfills the desire of he who fears Him, and hears his prayer."[44] This honor comes to him only through faith and not through any work. From this one sees clearly how a Christian is free of all things and over all things, so he requires no additional good work to make him pious and saved, rather faith brings him everything to overflowing. And if he were to be so foolish as to think to become pious, free, saved, or Christian through a good work, then he would lose his faith along with everything else, just like the dog that, while carrying a piece of meat in its mouth, snapped at its reflection in the water, and thereby lost both the meat and the reflection.[45]

17. You may ask, "What is the difference between priests and laymen in Christendom, if all are priests?" Answer: The little words "priest," "cleric," "spiritual," and so on, have suffered an injustice, for they have been transferred from the common masses to a small group, which one now calls the "spiritual estate."[46] The Holy Scripture makes no other distinctions than to term those who were learned or consecrated as *ministros, servos, oeconomos* (that is, attendants, servants, stewards) who are to preach Christ, faith, and Christian freedom to the others. For although we are all equally priests, yet we cannot all serve, enforce, and preach. Therefore St. Paul states in 1 Corinthians 4: "We want to be considered by the people as nothing more than attendants of Christ and stewards of the gospel."[47] But now from this stewardship has developed such a worldly, external, luxuriant, fear-provoking sovereignty and power, that the proper worldly power can in no way

---

44. Ps. 145:19.
45. This is a reference to one of Aesop's fables.
46. See note 27, above.
47. 1 Cor. 4:1.

compare, just as if the laity were something other than Christians. Hence the entire understanding of Christian grace, freedom, and faith, and everything that we have from Christ, including Christ Himself, are taken away; in return we have received many human laws and works, and have become wholly servants of the most incapable people on the earth.

18. From all of this we learn that it is not enough to preach if one speaks about Christ's life and work fleetingly and only as a history and historical chronicle, let alone if one is silent on these entirely, and only preaches on ecclesiastical law or other human law and doctrine. There are also many who preach and lecture about Christ in order to evoke sympathy with Him, to rage against the Jews, or thereby to act in some other even more childish manner. However, He should and must be preached such that faith grows and is preserved in me and you. This faith thereby grows and is preserved when I am told why Christ came, how one can use and enjoy Him, and what He has brought and given me. This occurs when one properly explains the Christian freedom that we have from Him; how we are kings and priests, powerful in all things; and that all that we do is pleasing to God's eyes and is heard by Him, as I have previously said. For when a heart hears Christ thusly, it must rejoice from its depths, receive consolation, grow tender toward Christ, and love Him in turn. This can never occur through laws or works. For who shall harm or frighten such a heart? Should sin and death befall it, yet it believes Christ's piety is its, and its sins are no longer its own, but are Christ's; thus in faith sins must disappear before the piety of Christ, as is stated above; and one learns with the apostle to defy death and sin, and say "Where now, O death, is your victory? Where now, death, is your spear? Your spear is sin. But praise and thank God, He has given us the victory through our Lord Jesus Christ; and death is drowned in His victory, etc."[48]

---

48. 1. Cor. 15: 55–57. Here Luther translates the Latin "stimulus," which can mean "sting," "spike," or "instrument of torment," as *Spieß*, or "spear"; whereas in his later German Bible he will use the word *Satchel*, or "sting," as will subsequent English-language versions. "Where, O death, is your victory? Where, O death, is your sting? The sting of death is sin, and the power of sin is the law. But thanks be to God, who gives us the victory through our Lord Jesus Christ."

The External Man

19. Now enough has been said of the internal man, of his freedom, and of the principal righteousness, which requires neither laws nor good works, and which can indeed be harmed if someone presumes to be justified in this way. Now we come to the second part, to the external man. Here we wish to answer all those who are vexed by the previous discussion and who are in the habit of saying: "Well, so then faith is all things and is alone sufficient to make one pious. Why then are good works commanded? For we would be in good shape without doing anything." No, my dear man, not so. It would indeed be fine if you were solely an internal man and became completely spiritual and internal, but this will not happen until Judgment Day. On earth there is, and will continue to be, only a beginning and an increase, which will be completed in the next world. Thus the apostle called it *primitias spiritus*, that is, the first fruits of the Spirit.[49] Therefore here should be repeated what was said above: "A Christian is a dutiful servant and is subject to everyone," or in other words, where he is free, he has to do nothing; where he is a servant, he must do all manner of things. How this happens we shall now see.

20. Although through faith a man is sufficiently justified internally, in regard to the soul, and has everything that he should have (though this faith and sufficiency always ought to increase until the next life), nevertheless he still remains on earth during this physical life and must rule his own body and interact with people. Here now works begin. He must not be idle; indeed, his body must be disciplined and trained with fasts, vigils, labors, and with every reasonable correction, such that it becomes obedient and in conformity to the internal man and to faith, rather than that it hinder or resist them, as is its way when it is not constrained. For the internal man is one with God, happy and merry for the sake of Christ, who has done so much for him, and all of his pleasure consists in also serving God in return, gratuitously and freely out of love. Yet he finds in his flesh a recalcitrant will, which wants to serve

---

49. Rom. 8:23: "And not only the creation, but we ourselves, who have the first fruits of the Spirit, groan inwardly while we wait for adoption, the redemption of our bodies."

the world and seeks only what pleases it. Faith cannot tolerate this, and gladly seizes it by the throat to subdue and bridle it. As St. Paul said in Romans 7: "I have a desire for God's will in regard to my internal man, yet I have another will within my flesh that wants to imprison me with sin."[50] Likewise, "I castigate my body and I discipline it into obedience, lest I myself, who should teach others, become reprobate."[51] Likewise in Galatians 5: "All who belong to Christ, crucify your flesh with its evil passions."[52]

21. But these same works must not be done in the opinion that man thereby becomes pious before God. Faith cannot tolerate this false opinion, for it alone is, and must be, the source of piety before God. Instead, works must be done in the opinion that thereby the body is made obedient and purified of its evil passions, and the eye only looks at evil passions in order to drive them out. For while, through faith, the soul is pure and loves God, she also desires that all things be pure, especially her own body, and that everyone love and praise God along with her. Thus it happens that a man, on account of his own body, cannot go idle but must practice many good works because of it and in order to constrain it. And yet works are not properly good, nor make him pious and righteous before God, rather he does them gratuitously and freely out of love, in order to please God; thereby not seeking or attempting anything else from them, than that they please God, whose will he gladly does to the best of his abilities. From this, then, everyone can determine the manner and have the discretion to mortify his own body, for he may fast, perform vigils, and labor insofar as he sees it necessary for his body in order to subdue its wantonness. Others, however, those who think to become pious with works, they pay no heed to mortification, rather they look only to works and think that if only they do many and great ones, this is well done and makes them pious; sometimes in the process they even damage their minds and ruin their

---

50. Rom. 7:22–23: "For I delight in the law of God in my inmost self, but I see in my members another law at war with the law of my mind, making me captive to the law of sin that dwells in my members."

51. 1 Cor. 9:27.

52. Gal. 5:24.

bodies. Yet it is a great folly and misunderstanding of Christian life and faith for them to intend to become pious and saved through work, without faith.

22. To give several analogies, one should consider the work of a Christian—who is justified and saved through his faith, and gratuitously by the sheer grace of God—just as if it were the same as the work of Adam and Eve in paradise. On this it is written in Genesis 2, that God placed the man He had created in paradise, so that he should labor and tend the same.[53] Now Adam was created by God as pious and good, without sin, such that he did not need to become pious and justified through his labors and tending. Yet so that he did not go idle, God gave him something to do: plant, cultivate, and safeguard paradise. These were purely free works, done for no other purpose than solely to please God and not in order to gain the piety which he already had, and which naturally would also have been inherited by all of us.[54] The works of a believing man are like this; through his faith he is once again placed in paradise and created anew. No work is required to make him pious; instead, solely to please God, he is ordered to do such free work so that he does not go idle and in order to exercise and safeguard his body.

Likewise, when a consecrated bishop consecrates churches, confirms, or otherwise practices his official work, these same works do not make him into a bishop. Indeed, if he were not already consecrated a bishop, none of these same works would be valid and they would be pure fool's work. Thus a Christian who, consecrated through faith, does good works will not become a better or more consecrated Christian through them (for they do nothing to increase faith). Indeed, if he did not already believe and was not a Christian, then all of his works would count for nothing, but would instead be purely foolish, wanton, damnable sins.

23. Thus these two sayings are true: "Good, pious works never make a good pious man, but a good pious man does good pious works. Evil works never make an evil man, but an evil man does evil

---

53. Gen. 2:15.
54. I.e., had Adam and Eve not sinned.

works." Therefore, the person must always be good and pious first, before all of his good works, and good works follow and proceed from the pious, good person. Just as Christ says: "An evil tree bears no good fruit. A good tree bears no evil fruit."[55] Now it is clear that the fruit does not bear the trees, neither do the trees grow on the fruit, but the other way around; the trees bear the fruit, and the fruit grows on the trees. Now just as the trees must precede the fruit, and the fruit does not make the trees either good or evil, but the trees make the fruit, so too must a man first be pious or evil as a person before he does good or evil works; his works make him neither good nor evil, rather he does good or evil works. We see the same thing in all trades. A good or evil house does not make a good or evil carpenter, but a good or evil carpenter makes an evil or good house. No work makes a master craftsman, whatever the work may be, but as the master is, so too is his work. The work of man is the same; how he stands in faith or unbelief determines if his works are good or evil, not the other way around, that how his works stand determines if he is pious or believing. Just as works do not make one believing, neither do they make one pious; but just as faith makes one pious, so it also makes one do good works. So then works make no one pious, and a man must first be pious before he works. Thus it is clear that faith alone, by sheer grace and through Christ and His word, makes a person sufficiently pious and saved. And that no work, no commandment, is necessary for a Christian's salvation, rather he is free of all commandments; and everything he does, he does out of sheer freedom, gratuitously, not seeking from it any benefit or salvation but only to please God; for he is already satisfied and saved through his faith and God's grace.

24. On the one hand, for he who is without faith, no good work is conducive toward piety and salvation; on the other hand, no evil work will make him evil and damned. But unbelief, which makes the person and the tree evil, does evil and damned works. Therefore if one will be pious or evil, one begins not with works but with faith. As the wise man says: "The beginning of all sin is to fall away from God and not to

---

55. Matt. 7:18.

trust Him."[56] Christ also teaches how one must not begin with works, and says: "Either make the tree good and its fruit good, or make the tree evil and its fruit evil,"[57] as if He were saying: "Whoever wants to have good fruit must first begin with the tree and plant it well." Thus whoever then wants to do good works must not begin with works, but with the person who shall do the works. No one makes the person good, however, for faith alone does this; and no one makes him evil, for unbelief alone does this. It is quite true that, in men's eyes, works make someone pious or evil, that is, they indicate externally who is pious or evil. As Christ says in Matthew 7: "From their fruits you shall know them."[58] Yet this is all appearances and external. Such an error of appearances is made by many people who then write and teach how one should do good works and so become pious. Yet they never think of faith, but, one blind man always leading another, carry on martyring themselves with many works and yet never coming to proper piety; of which St. Paul says in 2 Timothy 3: "They have an appearance of piety, but the foundation is not there; they go out and learn forever and ever, and yet never come to an understanding of true piety."[59] Now whoever does not want to err with the same blindness must look farther than works, commandments, or teaching on works. He must look within the person for all the things that make him pious. He will not, however, become pious and saved through commandments and works, but through God's word (that is, through His promise and grace) and through faith. His divine honor consists in this, that He saves us not

---

56. Luther refers here to the Book of Ecclesiasticus, also known as the Book of the All-Virtuous Wisdom of Jesus ben Sira (hence the reference to "the wise man"), or simply as Sirach. This book was accepted by the Catholic Church (and made officially canonical after 1546) but was rejected by Luther and most Protestants as apocryphal (though still worthy of citation and study). Here he cites Ecclus. 10:12–13: "The beginning of human pride is to forsake the Lord; the heart has withdrawn from its Maker. For the beginning of pride is sin, and the one who clings to it pours out abominations. Therefore the Lord brings upon them unheard-of calamities, and destroys them completely."

57. Matt. 12:33.

58. Matt. 7:20.

59. 2 Tim. 3:5,7.

through our works, but through His gracious word, gratuitously and from sheer mercifulness.

25. From all this it is easy to understand the ways in which good works are to be condemned and not condemned, and how one should understand all doctrines that teach good works. For where these contain the false stipulation and the perverse opinion that we become pious and saved through works, then already such works are not good and are completely damnable, for they are not free and blaspheme the grace of God, who alone makes us pious and saved through faith. This is something works cannot accomplish, yet they presume to be able to do it and thereby usurp grace in its work and honor. Therefore we do not condemn good works for their own sake, but for the sake of this same evil addition and false, perverse opinion, which makes them only appear good; and yet they are not good; they deceive themselves and everyone else, just like ravening wolves in sheep's clothing.[60] Yet this same evil addition and perverse opinion about works is invincible where there is no faith. Until faith comes and destroys it, it must remain within those who believe they are sanctified by works. Nature is not able to drive it out by itself. Indeed, nature also does not recognize it, but considers it as a precious, holy thing, and that is why so many are thereby led astray. For this reason, although it is certainly good to write and preach on contrition, confession, and satisfaction,[61] this is certainly a purely devilish, seductive teaching if one does not then continue on to faith. One must not preach on one type of God's words alone, but on both of them. One should preach the commandments to frighten sinners and to reveal their sin, such that they are contrite and are converted. But it should not stop there. One must also preach the other word, the assurance of grace, to teach faith, without which the commandments, contrition, and everything else happen in vain. There are indeed still preachers who preach contrition of sin and grace, but they do not explain the commandments and assurance of God in order to teach

---

60. Matt 7:15: "Beware of false prophets, which come to you in sheep's clothing, but inwardly are ravenous wolves."

61. The three parts of the church's sacrament of penance.

from where and how contrition and grace come. For contrition flows from the commandments, faith from the assurances of God; and so the man who is humbled and brought to awareness through fear of God's commandments, is justified and raised up through faith in the divine word.

Man's Relationship to Man

26. All this has concerned works in general and those that a Christian should practice for his own body. Now we shall say more on works that he does for other men. For a man does not live in his body alone, but also among other men on earth. Therefore he cannot be without works in relation to them; he must speak with them at some point and have dealings with them, even though no such work is necessary for his piety and salvation. Therefore in all his works his thoughts should be free and directed only so that he thereby serves and benefits other people. He should conceive of nothing else than what is necessary for the other. This, then, is a true Christian life, where faith undertakes work with passion and love, as St. Paul teaches in Galatians.[62] For to the Philippians, whom he had taught that they had every grace and sufficiency through their faith in Christ, he also taught further, saying: "I admonish you by all the consolation that you have in Christ, and all the consolation that you have from our love for you, and all the fellowship that you have with all spiritual pious Christians, that you would completely gladden my heart by henceforth wanting to be of one mind, each one bearing love toward the other, each one serving the other, and everyone paying heed not to himself or to his own affairs, but to others and what is necessary for them."[63] Behold, Paul clearly portrayed there a Christian life, that all works should be directed toward the good of the neighbor, because everyone has enough for himself in his faith, and all other works and life are superfluous for him, so he may thereby serve his neighbor

---

62. Gal. 5:6: "For in Christ Jesus neither circumcision nor uncircumcision counts for anything; the only thing that counts is faith working through love."
63. Phil. 2:1–4.

freely out of love. In addition, Paul brings up Christ as an example and says: "Be of the same mind that you see in Christ," who, although He was fully in divine form and had enough for Himself, and His life, acts, and suffering were not necessary for Him to become pious or saved, yet He emptied Himself of all of it and, taking the form of a servant, did and suffered everything, considering nothing but our best interests. And so although He was free, yet for our sakes He became a servant.[64]

27. Therefore a Christian, like Christ, his head, should be full, replete, and also content with his faith, always increasing the same, which is his life, piety, and salvation, and which gives him everything that Christ and God have, as is said above. And St. Paul says in Galatians 2: "What life I yet live in the body, I live in the faith of Christ, God's Son."[65] And even if he is now completely free, yet in turn he willingly makes himself an attendant to help his neighbors; going and dealing with them as God dealt with him through Christ, and all of it gratuitously, seeking nothing from it but God's good pleasure, and so thinking: "Well then, my God, through and in Christ, has given me—an unworthy, damned man, entirely without merit—the full wealth of all piety and salvation, utterly gratuitously and out of pure mercifulness, so that henceforth I require nothing more than to believe it is so. Ah, for such a Father, who has overwhelmed me with His greatly abundant goodness, I shall in turn freely, happily, and gratuitously do whatever will well please Him. And toward my neighbor I will also become a Christ, as Christ became for me, and will do nothing else than what I see is necessary, useful, and a blessing for him, although through my faith I have enough of everything in Christ." Behold, thus love and passion for

---

64. Phil. 2:5–8: "Let the same mind be in you that was in Christ Jesus, who, though He was in the form of God, did not regard equality with God as something to be exploited, but emptied Himself, taking the form of a slave, being born in human likeness. And being found in human form, He humbled Himself, and became obedient to the point of death—even death on a cross."

65. Gal. 2:20: "And it is no longer I who live, but Christ who lives in me. And the life I now live in the flesh I live by faith of the Son of God, who loved me and gave Himself for me."

God flows from faith, and from love a free, willing, happy life of serving one's neighbor gratuitously. For just as our neighbor suffers out of need and requires our surplus, we too suffered out of need for God and required His grace. Therefore, just as God helped us gratuitously through Christ, so we should do nothing else than help our neighbor through our body and its works. Thus we see how a Christian life is a highly noble life, though unfortunately it is now not only cast aside throughout the whole world, but is also no longer known or preached.

28. Thus we read in Luke 2 that the Virgin Mary, like all other women, went to the church after six weeks and was purified according to the law, even though she was not impure like them, nor accountable for the same purification, nor did she require it.[66] But she did it anyway, freely out of love, so that she did not scorn the other women, but instead remained with the masses. Thus St. Paul circumcised St. Timothy not because it was necessary, but so that he would not give Jews weak in faith a reason to have evil thoughts.[67] Yet on the other hand, he would not allow Titus to be circumcised, because they urged him to do so, saying he must be circumcised and it was necessary for salvation.[68] And in Matthew 17, when a tax was demanded from His disciples, Christ debated with St. Peter whether the children of the king were not free from paying taxes. And St. Peter said "Yes," yet He told him to go down to the sea and said: "So that we do not anger them, go down, take the first fish you catch, and in its mouth you will find a coin; give it for Me and you."[69] That is a fine example of this teaching, for Christ calls Himself and His disciples free children of the king who require nothing, and yet He willingly submits Himself, serves, and pays the tax. Now as much as this work was necessary for Christ and served toward His piety or salvation, so too are all His other works, and those of

---

66. Women were considered ritually impure for forty days after the birth of a boy child, eighty days after the birth of a girl (Lev. 12:1–5). Since Mary was thought to have conceived without sin, however, she was not impure. Luke 2:22.

67. Acts 16:3.

68. Gal. 2:3–4.

69. Matt. 17:24–27.

His Christians, necessary for their salvation.[70] Instead, all these services were done freely, for the sake and improvement of another. Thus all works by priests, monasteries, and religious foundations should also be done the same way, such that each one does the work of his estate or order[71] only to please another and to rule his own body. They should also provide and be an example to others, who also need to constrain their bodies, yet always being cautious that one does not intend thereby to become pious and saved, which is within the power of faith alone. In this way, St. Paul also stated in Romans 13 and Titus 3 that they should be subject to worldly authority and be prepared, not so that they thus become pious, but so that they might thereby freely serve others and the authorities, and do their will out of love and freedom.[72] Now whoever has this understanding can easily steer himself through the innumerable commandments and laws of pope, bishop, monastery, religious foundation, prince, and lord, which a number of mad prelates thus urge as if they were necessary for salvation, and call this the commandment of the church, however unjustly. For a free Christian speaks thusly: "I will fast, pray, do this and that, whatever is commanded, and not because I require this or because I will thereby become pious or saved; instead, for the sake of pope, bishop, the community, my fellow brother, or lord, I will provide an example, offer service, and suffer just as Christ did and suffered far greater things for my sake, even though it was much less necessary for Him. And even if tyrants act unjustly in demanding such things, yet it will not harm me as long as it is not contrary to God.

29. From this each man may form a sure judgment and make a distinction among all works and commandments, and also

---

70. In other words, not necessary at all.

71. His place in society or his monastic order. See also note 27, above.

72. Rom. 13:1–2: "Let every person be subject to the governing authorities; for there is no authority except from God, and those authorities that exist have been instituted by God. Therefore whoever resists authority resists what God has appointed, and those who resist will incur judgment"; and Titus 3:1: "Remind them to be subject to rulers and authorities, to be obedient, to be ready for every good work."

determine which prelates are blind, mad, or right-minded. For whichever work is not directed toward serving another or suffering under his will (insofar as he does not force one to act contrary to God) is not a good Christian work. As a result, I worry that few foundation churches, monasteries, altars, masses, and testaments are Christian; nor are the fasting and prayers specially made to a number of saints. For I fear that in all of this each one only seeks his own benefit and intends thereby to expiate his sins and to be saved. This all comes from ignorance about faith and Christian freedom, and a number of blind prelates urge the people in this direction and praise such ways, bedecking them with indulgences and never teaching faith. I advise you, instead, that if you wish to make an endowment, pray, or fast, do it not with the thought that you will do something good for yourself, but give it away freely so that other people may enjoy it. And if you do it for their good, then you are a proper Christian. What benefit to you are your property and those good works that are superfluous for you to rule over and care for your body, when you have enough in the faith through which God has given you all things? Behold, thus must God's goodness flow from one to the other and become common to all, so that each one also accepts his neighbor as if he were himself. This goodness flows into us from Christ, who has accepted us into His life, as if He were what we are. From us it should flow into those who require it. Indeed, I must offer to my neighbor even my faith and righteousness before God in order to cover his sins, take them onto myself, and act just as if they were my own, precisely as Christ has done for all of us. Behold, that is the nature of love, where it is true. And it is true where faith is true. For this reason the holy apostle said of love that it does not seek its own interests, but those of its neighbor.[73]

30. From all of this the conclusion follows that a Christian does not live within himself, but in Christ and his neighbor; in Christ through faith, in his neighbor through love. Through faith he rises above himself into God; from God he descends once again below himself through love, and yet remains always in God and divine love. Just as

---

73. 1 Cor. 13:5.

Christ said in John 1: "You will yet see heaven opened and the angels ascending and descending upon the Son of Man."[74] Behold, that is the proper, spiritual, Christian freedom, which makes the heart free of all sins, laws, and commandments, and which surpasses all other freedom as heaven surpasses the earth. May God grant that we properly understand and uphold this freedom. Amen.

---

74. John 1:51.

III. Catholic Opponents of Luther

Introduction

Martin Luther and other Protestant reformers are often credited with harnessing the new power of the printing press, a technology that allowed them to spread their message far and wide. Yet the success of the Protestant reformers was not a foregone conclusion, for many who read or heard the new ideas were repulsed, not enraptured, and Luther and his colleagues were not simply allowed to publish and preach unchallenged. Indeed, sixteenth-century Catholics were just as prolific as Protestants in publishing pamphlets, essays, sermons, and books to defend their own ideas and to attack the ideas and character of their enemies. Reformers and defenders of the old church thus engaged in a Europe-wide conversation, trading barbs, responding to perceived slurs or misrepresentations, and meeting argument for argument. Scripture was an important part of most such discussions, and was a flexible tool that could be wielded by clever theologians on both sides in order to sustain almost any argument. While there were many different points of attack made against Luther, however, the Catholic response tended to focus most on the question of authority. Luther's ideas and writings challenged the church's long monopoly on religious life, but also attacked the authority of church traditions, teachings, and practices, of church councils, of the priesthood, and of the pope himself. Luther's ideas, moreover, seemed to threaten the very social order and the relationship between church and state. This was not merely an intellectual exchange over obscure points of theology, in other words, but a struggle for the very survival of the church and of contemporary Christendom.

The universal language of this era was Latin, read and understood by every churchman, theologian, university professor, and learned layman, and that was the language used for much of the early back-and-forth among the contenders. However, just as Luther and the other reformers saw that the vernacular languages gave them a wider audience among those literate only in their own language, so too did the Catholics. They quickly began to issue vernacular translations of existing Latin works, and to produce new original works in German, French, English, and other European languages. Thomas Murner, for example, used the German vernacular for his famous satirical poem *The Great Lutheran Fool* (1522), a virulent personal attack on Luther and his followers meant for popular consumption. The humanist scholar Johann Cochlaeus, another early opponent of Luther, also printed numerous populist anti-Lutheran tracts and pamphlets in both Latin and German.[1]

In addition to polemical writings and public appeals or sermons, the church and its allies fought back against its critics in a number of other ways. Legal and ecclesiastical steps, such as excommunications, censorship, arrests, and even executions were sometimes effective, and war too would soon become an option for desperate governments. The church also attempted to silence any justified criticism through internal reform, a process sometimes termed the Catholic Reformation to distinguish it from the more direct Counter Reformation waged by church defenders. The major church council called at Trent in 1545 (and lasting until 1563) is a prime example of both branches of Catholic responses to the Protestant threat, for it not only offered denunciations of Protestant heresies, but also carefully specified Catholic doctrine and corrected some of the worst abuses within the church.

The broad character of the Catholic Church's attempt to defend itself from the existential threat of Protestantism thus involved a very large number of men (and some women) from throughout Europe. Yet the most famous, prolific, and well-read of these opponents of Luther and the Protestant Reformation was surely Johannes Eck (1486–1543). Born Johannes Maier in the small German town of Eck (later Egg) near Augsburg, Eck grew into a brilliant scholar and leading Catholic theologian. After an initial friendly interaction

---

1. For more on this topic, see David V. N. Bagchi, *Luther's Earliest Opponents: Catholic Controversialists, 1518–1525* (Minneapolis, 1991).

VERA IMAGO IOHANNIS ECKII.
THEOLOGIA D. ÆTATIS SVÆ. XLIII.

ECK EIN GROSSER FEIND CHRISTI WAR
HAT SEHR VERFOLGT DIE CHRISTLICH SCHAR
MIT SCHREIBEN YND YNNY CZEN GSCHWECZ
BRACHT ER DIE EINFELTIGEN INS NECZ
LIPRIGVND BÖS WAR ALL SEIN SIINN
VERGEBS IM GOT ER IST LANG HIINN.

Johannes Eck, portrait describing him as "a great enemy of Christ" by Balthasar
Jenichen, c. 1573.

with Luther, Eck reacted violently to the *Ninety-Five Theses*, which
seemed to him to be a direct attack on the authority of the church and
a throwback to the dangerous heresy of the Bohemian theologian Jan
Hus. This disagreement resulted in a bitter exchange of ideas, and in
1519 Eck and Luther met at a public disputation at Leipzig to resolve
the matter. Here Eck's clever debating skills won him additional fame
among church leaders, but did little to convince Luther or his supporters of the error of their ways—and did nothing to dampen Luther's
growing popularity in the empire. The Leipzig disputation also had
the counterproductive effect of further radicalizing Luther, for Eck not
only forced Luther to admit his support for certain heretical ideas once
espoused by Hus, but also to deny the authority both of popes and of
church councils.

Eck followed up the Leipzig disputation with numerous published works against Lutheran teachings, and was invited to Rome
to participate in a committee called to determine how to respond
to Luther. The result, which Eck guided, was the papal bull
Exsurge Domine (Arise O Lord), which banned Luther's works and

threatened excommunication unless he recanted his positions within sixty days. Eck was tasked with proclaiming this bull in Saxony and elsewhere in the empire, but faced considerable opposition from Luther's many supporters. Luther, firmly insistent of the rightness of his views, refused to recant within the allotted time, and his excommunication was finalized in January 1521. Eck then undertook a concerted written campaign against Luther, publishing work after work attacking his ideas. The most famous and popular of these was Eck's *Enchiridion Locorum Communium* (Handbook of Commonplaces), which was subsequently reprinted over a hundred times and in multiple languages. Eck also pursued other reformers, such as Philipp Melanchthon, Ulrich Zwingli, and the Strasbourg reformer Martin Bucer, and was still writing against the Protestants and defending Catholic doctrines at his death in 1543.

While the main battles against Martin Luther took place within the Holy Roman Empire and the German-speaking lands, Luther's ideas would also spread to Scandinavia, where they would eventually set long-term roots. England too would be strongly influenced by Luther. Indeed, in the fourteenth and fifteenth century England had already shown itself as fertile soil for a religious reform movement led by the theologian and philosopher John Wycliffe, who, like Luther and the Bohemian Jan Hus (who was inspired by Wycliffe's ideas), stressed the primacy of Scripture, advocated for the Bible to be written in the vernacular, and rejected clerical power and papal supremacy. By the time Luther published *On the Freedom of a Christian*, Wycliffe's movement, sometimes known as Lollardy, had long been suppressed in England, yet these ideas still had considerable support and presented a ready-made audience for Lutheran reform.

When news of Luther's growing popularity in the German lands reached England, therefore, government and church officials became concerned. They feared religious disorder and the return of Lollardy, but also wondered what Luther's ideas about faith alone would mean for public morality. If good behavior was not required for salvation, would the people not simply degenerate into immorality and license? Would Luther's "Christian liberty" not suggest to the ordinary man "the prospect of sinning with impunity and the freedom to commit all

John Fisher, Bishop of Rochester, by Hans Holbein the Younger, c. 1532–1535.

kinds of vice?"[2] In 1521, in response to this possible threat to English Catholicism and English society, Cardinal Thomas Wolsey, King Henry VIII's lord chancellor, ordered a ban on the importation and sale of all Lutheran works. King Henry VIII, meanwhile, had already begun work on his anti-Lutheran *Assertio Septem Sacramentorum* (Defense of the Seven Sacraments), which would be published later that year to great acclaim and popularity. Dedicated to Pope Leo X, it would also earn Henry the gratitude of the papacy and the honorary title "Defender of the Faith" (a title English monarchs still claim).

A major player in this English propaganda war against the specter of Lutheranism was John Fisher (1459–1535), a leading English scholar who served as bishop of Rochester from 1504 until his death. Aside from Thomas More, Fisher was perhaps Luther's most famous English opponent. He was especially well known for his *Assertionis Lutheranae Confutatio* (Refutation of Luther's Defense), a lengthy anti-Lutheran tract that systematically critiqued Luther's doctrine and

2. John Fisher, *Adversus Babylonicam Captivatatem*, 232, in Bagchi, *Luther's Earliest Opponents*, 127.

served as a direct rebuttal to a 1520 work of Luther's (that was itself a rebuttal of *Exsurge Domine*). The *Assertionis* was extremely popular, almost as popular as Henry VIII's *Defense*, and enjoyed multiple editions published throughout Europe. In addition to the *Assertionis* and many other polemical works, Fisher also preached two major public sermons against Luther, the first in 1521 and the second in 1526, both of which won praise for their clarity and forceful argumentation. Like Thomas More, Fisher too remained a loyal Catholic throughout his life. Unable to accept England's eventual break from the church and having alienated Henry VIII by opposing the king's divorce from Catherine of Aragon, he was executed in 1535 and later sainted by the Catholic Church as a martyr.

Johannes Eck, *Enchiridion*
or *Handbook of Commonplaces and Articles against the New Teachings Currently Wafting About*[1]

The most famous of Johannes Eck's works and the best-selling book against Luther in the sixteenth century is undoubtedly the Enchiridion Locorum Communium Adversus Lutherum et Alios Hostes Ecclesiae (*Handbook of Commonplaces against Luther and Other Enemies of the Church*). *The title of this work, which came out in 1525, was a conscious reply to the* Loci Communes *of Philipp Melanchthon, Luther's closest colleague and the leading Lutheran theologian of the day, and it was both a spirited attack on Luther and a fervent defense of Catholic teachings. Eck repeatedly revised and expanded the text over the years, with almost a hundred editions appearing before 1600, including major revisions in 1529, 1532, 1541, and 1572. In an effort to reach the German-speaking public, Eck also wrote a German version in 1530, which offered some new material and which expanded his attacks to include not just followers of Luther, but also of other contemporary reformers (all of whom he terms "new Christians"). Four additional German editions were published subsequently, as were French and Flemish translations. Interestingly, Eck visited England shortly before publishing the* Enchiridion, *and credited both Henry VIII and Fisher as sources of his material. The following selection is from one of Eck's German versions, which he hoped would have a more popular readership in the empire than the Latin. It was published in Augsburg in 1533 under the title* Enchiridion or Handbook of Commonplaces and Articles against the New Teachings Currently Wafting About, *and included thirty-four separate articles or sections on topics as varied as the primacy of the pope, the various*

---

1. This translation is based on the German text given in Johannes Eck, *Enchiridion, Handbüchlin gemainer stell unnd Artickel der jetzt schwebenden Neuwen leeren,* Faksimile-Druck der Ausgabe (Augsburg, 1533), edited by Erwin Iserloh (Münster: Aschendorff, 1980).

sacraments, feast days, priestly celibacy, the wars with the Turks, church titles, and the Anabaptists. Below are given the two sections, "On the Church and Her Authority" (Art. 1) and "On Faith and Good Works" (Art. 5), that most directly concern the issues raised by Luther in Freedom. *Here Eck strongly critiques Luther's claim in* Freedom *that the believer is his own priest, depends only on Scripture as his guide, and is thus free from the authority, rites, laws, and mediation of the church. He then attacks the very heart of Luther's message in* Freedom: *that we are saved through faith alone. Echoing many other contemporary Catholic critics of Luther's* Freedom, *Eck argued that this was utterly false. Indeed, he wrote, it was "wicked to think that mere faith is enough without good works."*

* * *

In Your Name Lord Jesus

1. On the Church and Her Authority

I. The Church is the Spiritual Body of Christ, United as a Spouse of Christ and Kingdom of Heaven[2]

Paul: "He has subjected all things under His feet, and has given Himself as head over the whole church, which is His body" (Eph. 1:22–23).[3]

i. The Church is a Body:

"I beg you, that you walk worthy of the calling by which you have been called, with all humility and meekness, with patience forbearing one another in love; being careful to keep the unity of the Spirit in the

---

2. I have inserted Roman numerals here and elsewhere in this article to better reflect and clarify Eck's organization.

3. All biblical citations shown are given in the original text, though I have clarified them by giving verse numbers, and standardized them to reflect the most common modern English naming and numbering conventions. Note that throughout this document I give literal translations of Eck's German-language Bible quotes, rather than using any specific English-language version of the Bible.

bond of peace. One body and one Spirit, even as you are called in one hope of your calling. One Lord, one faith, one baptism, one God and Father of us all, who is above us all, etc." (Eph. 4:1–6).

"One is my dove, my perfect one, she is the one of her mother, chosen by her that bore her" (Song of Sol. 6:9).

ii. The Church is a Spouse:

"A garden enclosed is my sister, my spouse; a garden enclosed, a fountain sealed" (Song of Sol. 4:12).

"Wives, be subject to your husbands, as to the Lord. For the husband is the head of the wife, even as Christ is the head of the church, He is a savior of His body. But just as the church is subject to Christ, so are wives to their husbands in all things. Husbands, love your wives, even as Christ has loved the church and has given Himself for her, that He might sanctify her, cleansing her by the pouring on of water in the word of life, that He might present it to Himself a glorious church, not having any spot or wrinkle, or any such thing, but that she should be holy and without blemish" (Eph. 5:22–27).

"And I, John, saw the holy city, the new Jerusalem, coming down from heaven, prepared by God as a bride for her husband" (Rev. 21:2).

"You are the body of Christ and members of one another" (Rom. 12:5; 1 Cor. 12:12). And much more can be found about the spiritual body in the same chapter and in Romans.

Thus the church is one. She is not outward and external as was the ark of Noah, which was a symbol of the one church, but outside this one church no one is saved, just as all men outside the ark perished (1 Pet. 3:20–21). Christ is not a bigamist: there is one church, that of the apostles and of us. Before Luther was born, there was the church, which had faith that there was a sacrifice within the Mass, there were seven sacraments, etc. This church was the bride of Christ, thus we should remain by this same church and not join in the new church of the wicked.[4]

Christ loved His bride, the church. Therefore He did not abandon her, neither for four hundred nor a thousand years. For how could the

---

4. I.e., the church of the reformers, such as Luther.

head abandon for so long His body? Indeed, since He left the synagogue, which was less beloved to Him, in physical captivity for only
seventy years at Babylon,[5] how could He then abandon His beloved
bride, the church, for a thousand years in the captivity of error and
false teaching?

iii. The Church is the Kingdom of Heaven:

"The kingdom of heaven is like a householder, who went out early in
the morning to hire laborers for his vineyard" (Matt. 20:1).

"The kingdom of heaven is like a man, a king who gave a wedding
for his son and who sent forth his servants to call those who had been
invited to the wedding" (Matt. 22:2–3).

"The kingdom of heaven is like ten virgins who took their lamps
and went forth to meet the bridegroom, and five of them were foolish"
(Matt. 25:1–2).

"The kingdom of heaven is like a net that was thrown into the sea
with which one gathered fish of all kinds. When it was full, they drew
it out and sat down next to it, and put the good into their vessels but
threw out the bad" (Matt. 13:47–49).

In all of these places the church is called the kingdom of heaven.
How then could error and falseness have now ruled for a thousand
years in this kingdom? The kingdom of heaven is a kingdom of truth.
It is obvious that God continually goes out to obtain day workers and
will until the end of the world. What then do the new Christians[6]
say? That the gospel has been set aside for four hundred years, and no
one was brought into the vineyard of God until Luther arrived? Here
it is also apparent that the church here on earth has been gathered
from the good and bad, for Christ says clearly that within her there are
prudent and foolish virgins, good and bad fish.

---

5. In the late sixth century B.C., after a rebellion against the Neo-Babylonian
ruler Nebuchadnezzar II, many leading Jews were sent into forced exile and captivity in Babylon and the First Temple at Jerusalem was destroyed. The Jews
were released roughly seventy years later after the Neo-Babylonians were con-
quered by the Persian emperor Cyrus, and on their return rebuilt the Temple.

6. The followers of Luther and other reformers.

II. The Church Does Not Err

The church does not err, not only because she always has her bride-groom, Christ, but also because she is governed by the instruction of the Holy Spirit.

"The church of the living God is the pillar and foundation of the truth" (1 Tim. 3:15).

"I have yet many things to say to you, but you cannot bear them now. Yet when the Spirit of Truth comes, He will teach you all the truth" (John 16:12–13). Here the new Christians, according to the gospel, must show us the instruction of the Holy Spirit, which is here promised to the church.

"You do not need anyone to teach you, but as His anointing teaches you of all things, and is true and is no lie" (1 John 2:27). Behold! The anointing of the Holy Spirit always teaches the church.

"Observe that I am with you every day until the completion of the world."[7]

Thus the church is a pillar of truth which, while Christ leads her and the Holy Spirit teaches her, does not err. Much less can she have erred for a thousand years, as the new Christians, Luther, Zwingli,[8] and Blarer[9] rave.

III. Just as the Church is One, So Too is There Unity Within the Church

"I beg you, brothers, by the name of our Lord Jesus Christ, that all of you speak the same thing, and that there be no divisions among you; but that you be perfectly joined together in the same thought and in the same mind" (1 Cor. 1:10). The new Christians do not hold to this. Not only are they split from us, but also among themselves, so that some of them are Lutheran, some are iconoclasts,[10] some are

---

7. Matt. 28:20. Here Eck does not give an in-text citation.

8. Ulrich Zwingli (1484–1531), pastor of the Grossmünster church in Zurich, was one of the greatest reformers of the era. He and Luther did not always see eye to eye.

9. Ambrosius Blarer (1492–1564) was a leading reformer in Constance, in southern Germany, and was strongly influenced by both Zwingli and Luther.

10. Those who destroy religious images.

against the sacraments, some are Anabaptists,[11] some are prophetic, and some even believe the soul dies, as with cattle.

"How long do you limp between two opinions? If the Lord is your God, follow Him; but if Baal, then follow him" (1 Kings 18:21). So how long do we Germans limp?

"No one can serve two masters" (Matt. 6:24). Thus no one can serve the church and also schism.

"God is not a God of disunity, but of peace, as I then teach in all churches of the saints" (1 Cor. 14:33). Indeed, it is even more to be supposed that God gives a spirit of proper understanding of the Scriptures to the church than to one particular man who divides himself from the church, just as do Luther, Osiander,[12] Zwingli, Hausschein,[13] and Schnepf.[14]

"Everything that is written, is written for our instruction. . . . May the God of patience and consolation grant you to be of one mind among one another, in accordance with Jesus Christ; so that you might with one voice glorify God the Father of our Lord Jesus Christ" (Rom. 15:4–6).

The church appeals to almighty, eternal God, by whose Spirit the whole body of the church is sanctified and ruled.

St. Paul concurs with this when he speaks of the Holy Spirit: "Be of the same mind toward one another. Do not consider lofty things, but condescend to the humble (the lowly)" (Rom. 12:16).

"If then there is any consolation in Christ . . . if there is any fellowship of the Spirit . . . then fulfill my joy, so that I am of one opinion, having the same love, being of one mind, and esteeming oneself just

---

11. Those who believed in adult baptism.

12. Andreas Osiander (1498–1552) was a leading theologian, mystic, and follower of Luther.

13. Johannes Œcolampadius (1482–1531), who changed his name from Hausschein into the Greek equivalent in the style of many contemporary humanist intellectuals, was a leading Protestant theologian known most for his work furthering the Reformation in Basel.

14. Erhard Schnepf (1495–1558) was a Lutheran theologian notable for his work as a professor at the Lutheran University of Marburg and for furthering the Reformation in Württemberg and elsewhere in Germany.

as another, and doing nothing out of quarrel or conceit" (Phil. 2:1–3). The new Christians hold to none of this. Some want to bring about new things, and neither one nor the other hold to the church.

"My people have committed two evils. They have forsaken Me, a fountain of living waters, and have dug for themselves broken cisterns that can hold no water" (Jer. 2:13). Thus the new Christians abandon the fountain of the church and dig collapsed cisterns of the heretics, of Wycliffe,[15] Hus,[16] the Waldensians,[17] etc.

In vain has God sent His son; in vain the Holy Spirit; in vain the apostles, martyrs, confessors, if the light of truth was to be revealed by Luther. Why then did God not send Luther in place of them all?

IV. The Prelates and Leaders of the Church Signify and are the Signified Church
"The king turned his face about, and blessed the entire church of Israel, and the entire church of Israel stood, etc." (1 Kings 8:14). See here "the church of Israel." And that this alone was the clear church is proclaimed in the lucid, clear text, which reads at the beginning: "Then were assembled all the elders of Israel with the princes of the tribes and leaders of the households of the children of Israel unto King Solomon" (1 Kings 8:1). Even more of this comes afterwards in their councils.

V. Objections of the New Christians
1. The faithful power (authority) of the Scriptures is greater than that of the church, for the church must be ruled according to the Scriptures, as the word of God yields to no one.

---

15. John Wycliffe (c. 1320–1384) was an early English reformer branded a heretic by the church.

16. Jan Hus (c. 1369–1415) was a Bohemian priest who, influenced by Wycliffe, attacked church teachings and the authority of the papacy. Many of his ideas were similar to those eventually adopted by Luther. Hus was burnt at the stake by church officials at Constance in 1415, sparking a full-scale rebellion of his followers in Bohemia.

17. A twelfth- and thirteenth-century religious movement named after the reformer Peter Waldo and declared a heresy by the church in 1215.

2. It is not permitted for the church or any man to go against the Scriptures.

3. One should not say that the church has decided something that the pope with the cardinals and bishops has decided. For the church is the congregation of all believers.

4. The church of God is solely within the Spirit, for she is something believed and is therefore concealed.[18]

5. Luther says he is of the church, and the church is with him. Therefore out of pride he calls himself an ecclesiastic. So too do Bucer,[19] Rottenacker,[20] Pellikan,[21] Linck,[22] etc.

VI. Reply of the Christians

To Point 1:

The Lord Christ wrote no book, nor did He command the apostles to write, but He commanded a great deal concerning the church. Therefore when He sent out the apostles He did not say "Go forth and write" but "Go forth and preach the gospel to all creatures" (Matt. 28:19).[23] For this reason the law of Moses was written on stone tablets, but the gospel in the hearts of the faithful. As St. Paul says: "You are the letter of Christ, prepared through our service, not written with ink but with the Spirit of the living God; not on stone tablets, but in fleshy tablets of the heart" (2 Cor. 3:2–3). This, about the heart, is also said by Jeremiah: "Behold, the day will come, and I will make a new covenant with the house of Israel and the house of Judah. Not according to the covenant that I made with your fathers, etc. . . . but this shall be the covenant that I will make with the house of Israel after those

---

18. See Luther, *Freedom*, §14.

19. Martin Bucer (1491–1551), a leading and extremely influential reformer in Strasbourg.

20. Konrad Sam (c. 1483–1533), born in the town of Rottenacker, helped further the reform movement in the city of Ulm.

21. Konrad Pellikan (1478–1556), born Konrad Kurscherer, was a Protestant theologian and reformer at Basel and Zurich.

22. Wenzeslaus Linck (1483–1547), a Lutheran theologian and reformer.

23. See also Matt. 24:14.

days, says the Lord; I will give My law within their natures and I will write it in their hearts; and I will be their God, and they shall be My people."[24]

The church is older than the Scriptures, for when the apostles began to preach there was no text of the gospel, also no epistles of Paul, and yet there was the church, sanctified in the blood of Christ.

Thus the apostles, without the Scripture of the New Testament, chose Matthew[25] and ordained seven deacons;[26] Peter caused Ananias and Sapphira to die.[27]

As the apostles were so diligent in proclaiming the word of God, and yet wrote little, it follows that they taught much more than they wrote, and both are equally credible. What they wrote is solely kept for the use of the church.

We do not know which Scriptures are credible and biblical without the confirmation of the church, for the biblical writers are members of the church.

Therefore to a heretic who wishes to discard the conventions and customs of the church, one should confront him in this way: "With which weapons do you wish to oppose church ordinances?" Then he would say: "With the validated biblical Scripture of the gospel and St. Paul's epistles." Then one must ask from where he knows that this gospel is biblical other than from the church? For why does he believe the Gospel of Mark, who was not an apostle and who, indeed, never even saw Christ (as many wished)? Why does he not accept the Gospel of Nicodemus, who saw and heard Christ, as John testifies (John 3:1–21)? Similarly, why do you believe in the Gospel of Luke the disciple and not in the Gospel of Bartholomew the apostle? Then along with St. Augustine, you should humbly confess the power of the church in the adoption of books—something Luther himself once taught: that the church may judge among the Scriptures—and even more in deciding the meaning of the Scriptures.

---

24. Jer. 31:31–33. For Müntzer's similar point see p. 109.
25. Acts 1:22–23.
26. Acts 6:3.
27. Acts 5:1–10.

Augustine, in *Against the Fundamental Epistle*: "I would not have believed the gospel unless the credibility of the church had moved me to do so."[28] See more on this later in Article 4.[29]

To Point 2:

The Scriptures teach: "Remember Saturday, that you keep it holy. Six days shall you work, and do all of your work, but the seventh day is the Sabbath of God your Lord, etc." (Exod. 20:8–10).[30] Yet by her own power and without the Scriptures the church shifted the observance of the Sabbath to Sunday, doubtless by the inspiration of the Holy Spirit.

Christ said to His disciples: "I am not come to destroy the law, but to fulfill it" (Matt. 5:17). Yet then the church of the apostles recognized that Jewish legal customs should cease and not be necessary (Acts 15).

Christ said to His disciples: "Go forth and teach all nations, baptizing them in the name of the Father, and of the Son, and of the Holy Spirit" (Matt. 28:19). Here Christ gave the form of baptism, which the church of the apostles and martyrs transformed, and baptized in the name of Jesus. As Peter says: "Repent, and be baptized every one of you in the name of Jesus Christ" (Acts 2:38). Luke says the same: "When they heard this, they were baptized in the name of Jesus" (Acts 19:5).

The Scriptures recognize: "It pleased the Holy Spirit and us to impose on you no further burden than these necessary things; namely that you abstain from things sacrificed to idols, and from blood, and from things strangled, and from fornication. If you keep yourself from these, you shall do well" (Acts 15:28). This is so clearly expressed in the Scriptures in the Acts of the Apostles, and yet later the church changed

---

28. Augustine, *Against the Fundamental Epistle of Manichaeus*, 5.6.

29. Article 4 of Eck's book is titled "On the Holy Spirit."

30. The Latin *sabbatum* or Hebrew *shabbath* was the seventh day of the week among the Hebrews—i.e., Saturday—Sunday being the first day of the week. Early Christians, however, changed Jewish practice by setting aside Sunday instead as their day of worship. Here Eck makes the point that the Sabbath day is technically Saturday when he translates this passage of Exodus as "Remember Saturday" instead of the usual "Remember the Sabbath day."

this through her own power, without the Scriptures, for we eat blood and things strangled. See Article 12 for more on this.[31]

And if it pleases the new Christians to live more according to the Scriptures than according to the ordinances of the Christian Church, then all baptized Jews would be bound to keep the law of Moses, for the Scriptures indicate that the apostles and other converts from Judaism lived that way. James and the elders said to Paul: "See brother, how many thousands of believers there are among the Jews, and they are all zealous for the law. And they have been told about you, how you teach all the Jews who live among the Gentiles to forsake Moses, saying that they should not circumcise their children, nor follow their customs. What then is to be done? It is necessary that the multitude come together, for they will learn that you have come. So now do what we tell you. We have four men who have made a vow. Take them and purify yourself with them, and give to them so that they might shave their heads, so they will all know that it is false what they have heard about you, but that you also follow the law and keep it" (Acts 21:20–24). Here St. Paul and St. James with many thousands lived according to the law. If the new Christians will now live according to this Scripture, so too must all converts from the Jewish life live according to Jewish custom. Where then is the freedom of the gospel?

To Point 3:

We confess that the church is the congregation of believers who are in the body of Christ. But when the leaders and most distinguished members of every estate regulate or establish something in a province or region, we say that the province or the land has made the law or the territorial ordinance. It is the same for the prelates and leaders of the church. They stand for the whole church, for they are there in the place of their subjects. For how else would the entire church be assembled? Christ said: "But if he will not hear you . . . then tell the church" (Matt. 18:16–17). Now if one wanted to tell the church when Zwingli will not hear Luther on the sacraments, he would have to trek throughout the world. Chrysostom interprets this correctly, saying

---

31. Article 12 of Eck's book is titled "On Human Statutes and Laws."

of the church that it is the prelates and leaders of the church.[32] The text also supports this, for where Christ spoke of the church that one should hear, immediately thereafter He gave the apostles the power to bind and loose; thereby He indicated that they are the church of which He spoke.[33]

"If you perceive a difficult and ambiguous judgment between blood and blood, cause and cause, leper and leper, and you see that within your gates the words of the judges vary, then arise and go up to the place that the Lord your God shall choose. And you shall come to the priests of the race of Levi, and to the judge who shall be there at the same time, and you will enquire of them, and they shall show you the truth of the judgment, and you shall do everything that they shall say, who are the leaders in the place that God shall choose, and they shall teach you according to His law, and you shall follow their opinion and sentence; you shall not turn aside either to the right or the left hand. But he who would be presumptuous and will not be obedient to the bidding of the priest who serves the Lord your God at that same time, by the verdict of that judge the man dies, and you shall remove the evil from Israel. And all the people who shall hear this shall fear, so that afterwards no one shall swell up with pride" (Deut. 17:8–13). See the power of the Mosaic priest. How much greater do you think is the power of the priest of the gospel? Note well the punishment of the disobedient.

"And when Paul and Barnabas had no small disagreement against some propositions, they decreed that Paul and Barnabas and some others of the other side should go to Jerusalem to the apostles and priests (or elders) about this question" (Acts 15:2). See how they fulfilled the commandment of Deuteronomy 17? See also who was there as the church. Not the congregation of all believers, but the apostles and elders. They represented and signified the entire church.

To Point 4:

If the church is secretly concealed, as Luther proposes, how then did Christ command us to tell the church? To hear her when one of us

---

32. John Chrysostom (c. 347–407), a church father. Here Eck is referring to Chrysostom's *Homilies on Matthew*, 60:2.
33. Matt. 18:17–18.

sins (Matt. 18:17)? Similarly, the church is the body of Christ, and Christians are her members (Rom. 12:5). Now tell me, Luther or Rottenacker, if they are also concealed and there is only an imaginary church? On this Paul says: "You are the body of Christ, and members through one another" (1 Cor. 10:16–17; 1 Cor. 12:27; Eph. 1:23; Eph. 5:30; Col. 1:18). It is the character of the heretics that they have pits, caves, and hiding places; the church sets her candle upon a candlestick (Luke 11:33). The church is shown to Christians in the councils, in the Roman See,[34] in bishops and prelates of individual churches.

Were the church solely imaginary (mathematical), the brother of Paul[35] would not be praised through all the churches (2 Cor. 1:1). David would not say: "With you is my praise in a great church" (Ps. 21:26).[36] He would not say: "They shall exalt Him in the congregation of the people, and they shall praise Him in the seat of the elders" (Ps. 106:32).[37] See for this Augustine on the First Epistle of John, the first tractate at the end.[38] Yet it is true that the bond of the church in faith and love is spiritual and concealed.

To Point 5:

What Luther says here is said by all heretics. For this reason Augustine conducted a fierce invective against the Donatists,[39] who wanted to force the Christian congregation of the church into the narrow corner of a few heretics who thought that the church was with them

---

34. The papacy.

35. Timothy.

36. Here Eck uses the numbering of the Psalms as given in the Latin Vulgate, which was the most common translation of the Bible used in the Middle Ages (and which had the same enumeration of the Psalms as the older Greek Septuagint). Most Protestant bibles use instead the numbering of the Psalms found in the Hebrew-language Masoretic Text. Thus in Protestant bibles this would be Ps. 22:26.

37. Ps. 107:32 in the Masoretic Text.

38. St. Augustine of Hippo, *Homilies on the First Epistle of John*, 1:12–1:13.

39. The Donatists were a Christian sect who disagreed with the official church over the validity of sacraments celebrated by unfit priests (among other things), and who argued that they alone represented the true church.

alone. See for this the true knight of the faithful Doctor Cochlaeus in the book on the power and eminence of the church.[40]

5. On Faith and Good Works

Where it is demonstrated that faith alone is insufficient without works, and that works are something that, out of divine grace, one undertakes for recompense.

"Whatever your hand is able to do, do that work continuously or constantly" (Eccles. 9:10).

"Drink your wine with joy, for your work pleases God (Eccles. 9:7).

"Therefore as long as we have time, let us do good works," for the night is coming, and no one may work therein (Gal. 6:10).

All of us were in the vineyard not with a slumbering faith, but so that we labored and worked (Matt. 20).

"God shall give to he who understands the reward for his work" (Wisd. of Sol. 10:17).[41]

"He who fears God, believe Him; and your reward shall not be in vain" (Ecclus. 2:8).[42]

John: "Their works will follow them" (Rev. 14:13).

"Therefore, you brethren, be more diligent so that you, through your good works, will make certain your election and calling" (2 Pet. 1:10).

St. Paul: "For we must all appear before the judgment seat of Christ; that everyone may receive the things (here understand this as

---

40. Johann Cochlaeus (1479–1552), a German humanist and bitter opponent of Luther. The book Eck mentions here is *De Authoritate Ecclesiae et Scripture* (On the Authority of the Church and Scripture) (1524), written to refute Luther's teachings on this matter.

41. The book known as Wisdom, or the Wisdom of Solomon, is one of the books of the Old Testament that was not part of the Hebrew Scriptures but was accepted by the Catholic Church (and made officially canonical after 1546). It was considered as apocryphal and non-canonical by Luther and other Protestants (though still worthy of citation and study).

42. The Book of Ecclesiasticus, also known as Sirach, was also rejected as apocryphal by Luther and most Protestants.

"work") of the body, according to what he has done, whether it be good or bad" (2 Cor. 5:10).

"God is not unrighteous, that He forgets your work and labor, which you have taken up out of love" (Heb. 6:10).

Athanasius:[43] "And those who have done good works will enter into eternal life, and those who have done evil into eternal fire."[44]

St. Paul: "God will render to every man according to his works" (Rom. 2:6). St. Paul: "Honor and glory and peace to every man who does good" (Rom. 2:10).

St. Paul: "Not those who are hearers of the law are just before God, but those who do the law shall be justified" (Rom. 2:13).

Christ: "If you will enter into life, keep the commandments" (Matt. 19:17).

Christ: "Not everyone who says unto Me, 'Lord, Lord,' shall enter into the kingdom of heaven; but he that does the will of My Father" (Matt. 7:21).

Christ: "He who has My commandments and keeps them, he is it who loves Me" (John 14:21).

Christ: "You are My friends if you do what I have commanded you" (John 15:14).

St. John says: "Whoever says he knows God, and does not keep His commandments, he is a liar and there is no truth in him" (1 John 2:4).

"Make way for every work of mercy: for everyone receives according to his works" (Ecclus. 16:14).

St. Paul: "You shall not forget sharing and doing good, for by such sacrifices God is served" (Heb. 13:16).

St. John: "My reward is with me; to repay everyone according to his works" (Acts of John 113).[45]

Christ says: "Rejoice and be glad, for your reward is great in heaven" (Matt. 5:12).

---

43. St. Athanasius of Alexandria (c. 296–373), bishop of Alexandria, leading theologian, and also a church father and doctor.

44. Athanasius, *De Incarnatione Verbi* (On the Incarnation of the Word), §56.

45. From the apocryphal Acts of John.

St. Paul: "For me to live is Christ, and to die is gain" (Phil. 1:21). If it is a gain, so is it also earned.

I. Faith without Work is in Vain and Futile
St. James: "What use is it, my brethren, if someone says he has faith, and yet does not have works? Can faith then save him?" (James 2:14). And later: "Faith, if it does not have works, is dead in itself" (James 2:17). And later: "Will you then know, O vain man, that faith without works is dead?" (James 2:20). And previously: "You believe that there is one God; you do well: the devils also believe, and tremble" (James 2:19).

It is not enough to believe. It is not enough that the eyes of the blind man be coated with clay. He must also go to the pool of Siloe, that is, he must also purify himself through good works (John 9).

"If I should have all faith, so that I could remove mountains, but do not have love, I am nothing" (1 Cor. 13:2). From these words of St. Paul, Augustine proved that faith does not necessarily have love attached to it (*Trinitate*, 15:18).[46]

St. Paul: "Let us do good to all, especially to those who are of the household of faith" (Gal. 6:10).

St. Paul: "I have fought a good fight, I have finished my course, I have kept the faith: henceforth there is reserved for me a crown of righteousness, which the Lord, the righteous judge, shall give me on that day" (2 Tim. 4:7–8).

St. Paul: "For it is given to you, for Christ, not only that you believe in Him, but also that you suffer for His sake" (Phil. 1:29).

St. Paul: "That you walk worthily, and please God in all things, and be fruitful in every good work, and increase in all knowledge" (Col. 1:10).

II. Works are Meritorious
"Call the laborers, and give them their reward" (Matt. 20:8). And previously: "Whatever is right I will give you" (Matt. 20:4).

"I shall be your exceeding great reward" (Gen. 15:1).

"Everyone shall receive his reward according to his labor" (1 Cor. 3:8).

"Your work shall be rewarded" (2 Chron. 15:7).

---

46. St. Augustine of Hippo, *De Trinitate* (On the Trinity), c. 417.

"The godless man performs a deceitful work, but to him who sows righteousness shall be a true reward" (Prov. 11:18).

"I have inclined my heart to perform righteousness, on account of the recompense" (Ps. 118:112).[47]

III. Objections of the New Christians

1. "The righteous lives by faith" (Rom. 1:17), therefore he does not live by works.

2. "He who believes in the Son of God shall not be damned" (1 John 5:13).

3. "Do you believe that I am able to do this? . . . According to your faith be it done to you" (Matt. 9:28–29).

4. "Abraham believed in God, and it was accounted to him as righteousness" (Gen. 15:6).

5. "Whoever hears My word and believes in Him who sent Me has eternal life" (John 5:24).

6. "Your faith has saved you" (Matt. 9:22). Works are of hypocrites.

7. Love is a fruit of faith, therefore faith is alone sufficient.[48]

8. St. Paul's epistles to the Romans and Galatians contend that man is justified without works (Gal. 5:4–6).

IV. Reply of the Faithful

To Point 1 [and 8]:

Here it is obvious that it is true what St. Augustine says: this heresy (for it is ancient) arose from the words of St. Paul falsely understood. For as Habakkuk[49] and Paul said that "the righteous lives by faith,"[50] so faith is the foundation and basis of the spiritual structure. As St. Paul said: "Faith is the foundation of things that one hopes for" (Heb. 11:1). Therefore he speaks of faith as being the origin and beginning, for the perfection of the Christian life is fulfilled through love.

---

47. Ps. 119:112 in the Masoretic Text.

48. In the Latin version of this text Eck notes that this objection is taken by the Lutherans from Augustine's *On Faith and Works.*

49. A Hebrew prophet and author of the biblical Book of Habakkuk.

50. Hab. 2:4; Rom. 1:17; Gal 3:11.

Furthermore, while St. Paul says that the righteous lives by faith, Luther adds "alone" to "by faith."[51] With this addition, "alone," he falsifies the text and shreds it, violating his own [principles] and God's commandment: "One shall add nothing to it, etc."[52]

To Point 2:

Faith fully employs the Scriptures, is included within it, and adheres to God through love, as St. Augustine explains (Tract. 10, John 2).[53] The young theologians call this a formed or living faith. This is clear from Paul: "In Christ Jesus neither circumcision nor uncircumcision avails anything; but faith that works by love" (Gal. 5:6). Note that Paul does not allow that all faith suffices, only a beneficent and loving faith.[54]

To Point 3:

This is repudiated by the previous answer. However I do not deny that an unloving faith may also earn something temporal from God, for the Romans, on account of their virtue, earned the rulership of the entire world, as Augustine says (*De Ci. Dei*, 5:15).[55]

To Point 4:

St. James gives an answer: "Was not Abraham, our father, justified by works, as he offered up his son on the altar? Do you see that faith cooperated with works, and faith was made perfect by works?" (James

---

51. Luther, in his translation and use of Romans 1:17, adds the word "alone" to Paul's statement, "The one who is righteous will live by faith." This was to emphasize his point, but Eck and other critics of Luther rightly note that this addition alters the original and adds Luther's own words to the biblical text.

52. Deut. 4:2; Deut. 12:32; Rev. 22:18; Prov. 30:6.

53. Augustine, *Tractates on the Gospel of John*, Tractate 10 (on John 2:12–21).

54. Luther responded to this common Catholic criticism (which harkens back to the Thomist stress on the importance of love or charity in completing faith) in *Freedom*, but addressed the issue more specifically in a sermon on 1 Corinthians 13. See John Nicholas Lenker, ed., *The Sermons of Martin Luther: The Church Postils*, vol. 7 (Grand Rapids, MI: Baker Book House, 1982), 119–132.

55. St. Augustine of Hippo, *De Civitate Dei contra Paganos* (The City of God against the Pagans).

2:21–22). And later:"Do you see that a man is justified by works and not by faith alone?" (James 2:24). For this reason the angel spoke to Abraham:"Because you have done this thing, etc." (Gen. 22:16).

To Points 5 and 6:

As with the others, I say that he is a slanderer who says works belong to hypocrites. Why then has Christ commanded: "So let your light shine before men, so that they may see your good works and glorify your Father who is in heaven"?[56] Why are the new Christians so troubled by good works? I will say that they boast about the gospel and call themselves evangelical with their mouths, but one sees no evangelical work within them.

To Point 7:

Here Luther shreds the Scriptures, for love is not the fruit of faith, but of the Spirit, just as faith is also called a fruit of the Spirit by Paul (Gal. 5:22–23).

The majority of the new Christians see that they cannot withstand the powerful sayings of the Scriptures. They also note how wicked it is to think that mere faith is enough without good works—something that repulses our holy beliefs; for there could be no worse faith in the world. The Christian faith, but also the Jews, Turks, Tatar, etc., all require and teach good works, good morals, and virtues, and out of prudence all teach sin and vice and all command good works. Only the Lutheran faith is an exception.

Now they have therefore begun to distinguish two types of faith. One they call a historical or historic faith, the other a love-rich or benevolent faith (Œcolampadius, *Demegoria*).[57]

---

56. Matt. 5:16.

57. Here Eck may be referring to a chapter within Œcolampadius' 1524 commentaries on 1 John.

John Fisher, *Sermon against the Pernicious Doctrine of Martin Luther*[1]

In 1521, as part of the English monarchy's organized campaign against Luther and as a display of loyalty to the Catholic Church, Cardinal Thomas Wolsey arranged a public ceremony for the promulgation of Exsurge Domine *(the papal bull condemning Luther). The ceremony, held on Sunday, 12 May, was a huge affair, attended by numerous English clergy, foreign dignitaries, and crowds of interested Londoners. Confiscated Lutheran books were burnt in a great bonfire, and Bishop John Fisher, renowned for his academic credentials and his sanctity, was tasked to present a public sermon suitable to the occasion. This sermon, directed "against the pernicious doctrine" of Luther, was subsequently published in both English and Latin, a copy of which was sent to the pope. In this sermon, Fisher's first point was to defend papal primacy and the authority of the church in establishing doctrines and practices. He did this by stressing the role of the Spirit of Truth, or the Holy Spirit, as a guiding force in the church. Luther's failure, Fisher argued, was that he refused to accept this Spirit or to see that it abides forever within the church and ensures that the church shall never fall into error and heresy. Fisher also attacked Luther's argument, expressed strongly in* Freedom, *that one is justified by faith alone, and he countered Luther's claim that Scripture alone, not Scripture along with the teachings and traditions of the church, is authoritative.*

* * *

<hr>

1. This selection was taken from the edition published in 1521, copy held by Cambridge University Library. For ease of reading I have modernized the English. I have also either cut Latin phrases that Fisher himself also translates, or given English translations for Latin phrases that Fisher does not translate.

Sermon of John, the Bishop of Rochester, Made against the Pernicious Doctrine of Martin Luther, within the Octaves of the Ascension by the Assignment of the Most Revered Father in God the Lord Thomas Cardinal of York and Legate *Ex Latere* from Our Holy Father the Pope.[2]

"When the Comforter shall come, whom I shall send to you, the Spirit of Truth who issues from My Father, He shall bear witness of Me."[3]

These words are the words of our Savior Christ Jesus in the Gospel of John and read in the service of this present Sunday.

Very often when the day is clear and the sun shines bright, in some quarter of the heavens a thick black cloud arises that darkens all the face of the heavens, shadows us from the clear light of the sun, stirs up a hideous tempest, makes a great lightning, and thunders terribly, so that weak souls and feeble hearts are put into a great fear and made almost desperate for lack of comfort.

In like manner it occurs in the church of Christ. When the light of faith that shines from the spiritual sun, almighty God, has been clear and bright for a good season, there has often arisen some black cloud of heresy and stirred such a tempest, and made such a lightning, and so terribly thundered that many a weak soul has thereby gone awry.

Lo, such a cloud was Arius,[4] who stirred up so great a tempest that many years afterwards it vexed the church of Christ. And after him came many other like clouds, such as Macedonius, Nestorius, Eutyches, Helvidius, Donatus, Jovinianus, Pelagius, John Wycliffe,[5] with many others who sore tempested the church, every one of them in his time. Such heretics St. Jude in his epistle calls "clouds without water,

---

2. A legate *ex latere* or papal legate is a representative of the pope, fully empowered by him to handle specific church matters. Cardinal Thomas Wolsey (1473–1530) was also archbishop of York and King Henry VIII's chief adviser and lord chancellor.

3. John 15:26. The passage refers to the Holy Spirit.

4. Arius (c. 250–336) was a church leader from North Africa who argued that Jesus was not the same as God the Father, but was created later and is thus inferior. His teachings were declared heretical at the Council of Nicaea in 325.

5. All men whose teachings were declared heretical.

which are carried about by wind."[6] That is to say clouds without the moisture of grace, which are moved with the blast of wicked spirits. And now another such cloud is raised aloft, one Friar Martin Luther, who has stirred up a mighty storm and tempest in the church, and has thrown a shadow over the clear light of many Scriptures of God. And he issues from himself a perilous lightning, that is to say a false light of wrong understanding of Scripture, which emerges not from the Spirit of Truth, but from the spirit of error and from the spirit of this tempest of his most perilous heresy. Furthermore he thunders terribly against the pope's authority, against the general councils, against the traditions and ordinances left to us by the apostles, against the doctrine of the fathers and doctors of the church.[7]

Our Savior Christ, therefore, foreseeing by His divine providence that many such pestilent clouds and tempests would arise to the great trouble and vexation of His church, promised out of the tender love and infinite charity that He bears for our mother, the holy church, that after He had ascended to His Father, He would send to her the Holy Spirit of God, the Spirit of Truth, who would abide with her forever to establish for her from time to time every truth to which both she and every child of hers, which is to say every true Christian man, should give assured faith; and finally to be for her a veritable comforter in all such storms, according to the beginning of this gospel recounted above: "When the Comforter shall come, whom I shall send to you, the Spirit of Truth who issues from My Father, He shall bear witness of Me." This holy gospel graciously offers to us four excellent instructions against these dangerous tempests of heresy whenever they happen to arise, but especially against this most pernicious tempest that Martin Luther has now stirred up.

The first three instructions, by God's leave and the help of this Holy Spirit, shall undermine three great grounds upon which Martin

---

6. Jude 1:12.

7. The title of "father of the church" is given to eminent scholars or leaders in the early church who had special significance or influence. The title of "doctor of the church" is more restrictive, and is given only after sainthood to theologians whose great learning and writings have contributed significantly to church doctrine or theology.

establishes all his articles, and the fourth shall answer the defense that is made for him by his adherents, whereby many a weak soul is in peril.

But before we begin to make a declaration of them, we shall make our prayer to this Holy Spirit of Truth, that in this dangerous storm and perilous tempest He will stay our hearts with the testimony of His truth, that we do not falter in the Catholic doctrine of our holy mother church, but firmly believe such teaching as has been derived to us from our Savior Christ Jesus by His apostles and their successors, the holy bishops and fathers and doctors of the church. For this and for the grace necessary for you and for me, every person should say their devotion.

The First Instruction

The first instruction is offered to us from these first words of the gospel: "When the Comforter shall come, whom I shall send to you, the Spirit of Truth who issues from My Father." In these words is promised to us the Spirit of Truth to be our comfort in all doubtful opinions that may arise in Christ's church.

Touching this instruction I would do three things. First, I would show that the instructions of this holy gospel pertain to the universal church of Christ. Second, that the head of the universal church (by divine law) is the pope. Third, that Martin Luther (who divides himself from this head), does not have within him the Spirit of Truth.

For the first: Martin Luther cannot deny that this promise is made to the universal church and thereby we shall bind him by his own reason. He says in the book *On the Babylonian Captivity*:[8] "If we will affirm that any one epistle of St. Paul or any one place of his epistles does not pertain to the universal church of Christ, we take away all St. Paul's authority."

Now if this is true of the words of St. Paul, all the more is this true of the Gospels of Christ and of every place written in the same Gospels. In the universal church, then, this Holy Spirit of Truth rests and shall continue until the world's end. He shall abide in the universal

---

8. Martin Luther, *On the Babylonian Captivity of the Church*, 1520.

church forever[9] and He shall in every doubt teach us the truth.[10] So much for the first point.

Now for the second, where I said that the pope by divine law is the head of the universal church of Christ. When you see a tree standing upright upon the ground and its branches spread widely, full of leaves and fruit, if the sun shines clear, this tree makes a shadow. In this shadow you may perceive a figure of the branches, of the leaves, and of the fruit. Everything that is in the tree has something corresponding to it in the shadow. And on the contrary, every part of the shadow has something corresponding to it in the tree. A man's eye may lead him from every part of the tree to every part of the shadow, and again from every part of the shadow to every part of the tree that corresponds to it. Every man may point to any certain part of the shadow and say: This is the shadow of such a branch, and this is the shadow of such a leaf, and this is the shadow of the trunk of the tree, and this is the shadow of the top of the tree.

But so it is that the law of Moses and the governance of the synagogue of the Jews were but a shadow of the governance of the universal church of Christ. So said St. Paul: "The law had but a shadow of good things to come";[11] and to the Corinthians: "Now all these things happened unto them for examples." That is to say, all their governance was but a figure and shadow of the church."[12]

Now then to my purpose. In their governance, two heads were appointed, one under the other, Moses and Aaron, to conduct the people through the desert to the country that was promised them. We know that the people of the Jews were a shadow of the Christian people, and that their journey by the desert toward the country promised them was a shadow of our journey through this wretched world into the country of heaven. But Moses and Aaron, who were the heads of that people, what are they shadows of? Without doubt they must be the shadows of Christ and of his vicar St. Peter, who under Christ was also the head of Christian people.

---

9. John 14:16.
10. John 16:13.
11. Heb. 10:1.
12. 1 Cor. 10:11.

And you will see this more manifestly by three likenesses. First, Moses and Aaron, both of them, were priests. Moses was made so by God and Aaron made so by Moses at the commandment of God, to whom was committed the cure of the Jews in the absence of Moses. So Christ and St. Peter both were priests of the new law. Christ made so by His Father almighty God, as it is written of Him: "You are a priest forever according to the order of Melchisedech."[13] And Peter was made so by Christ, to whom He commissioned in His absence the cure of the Christian people, saying "Feed My sheep,"[14] feed, feed, feed. The second likeness is this. Moses was mediator between almighty God and Aaron for the causes of the people, and Aaron was mediator between Moses and the people touching the causes of God. So Scripture teaches in Exodus 4. Almighty God said unto Moses speaking of Aaron: "He shall speak in your stead unto the people, and you shall be for him in return in those causes that pertain unto God."[15] Will you see how Christ was the mouth of Peter toward almighty God? He said to St. Peter: "Simon, Simon, lo Satan has coveted greatly to sift you as a man sifts his wheat. But I have prayed for you to the intent that your faith does not fail; and you, once turned to the stable way, confirm your brethren."[16] See now here whether Christ was not the mouth of Peter when He promoted his cause before almighty God the Father, and prayed for him that his faith should not finally perish? And on the contrary, was not Peter the mouth of Christ, when he, converted to the true way, did confirm his brethren? Here note well what authority was given to Peter over them, to confirm all the others of his brethren in the stable way.

The third likeness is this. Moses ascended unto the mountain to speak with almighty God, and Aaron remained behind to instruct the people. Did not Christ likewise ascend unto His Father to the great mount of heaven? And to what extent, I pray you? St. Paul tells: "To appear before the face of almighty God for us"[17] and there to be our

---

13. Heb. 5:6.
14. John 21:17.
15. Exod. 4:16.
16. Luke 22:31.
17. Heb. 9:24.

advocate, as says St. John. And did not Peter remain behind to teach
the people, which our Savior committed unto his charge, just as Aaron
was left to do for the people of the Jews when Moses was above on the
mount with God?

Thus every man may see how that shadow and this thing agree
and answer one to another fully and clearly. But now let us pause here
a while. I will expound upon this figure further by another deed of
Christ in the Gospels. So it was that the Jews were tributaries to the
Romans, and for that tribute the head of every household paid a certain coin called a didrachma.[18] So when they who were the gather-
ers of this tribute came to St. Peter, our Savior bade him to go to the
sea, and told him that in a fish's belly there he should find a stater,
which was a double didrachma, and bade him to pay that to the gath-
erers, both for himself and for Christ.[19] Mark here that this tribute
was head money paid for those who were headless[20] and were gov-
ernors of households, and Christ commanded this to be paid for no
others but only for Himself and for St. Peter, and thereby satisfied the
entire amount. Join this fact of the gospel unto that figure before, and
what can be more evident to show that Peter under Christ was the
head of all the household of Christ? But yet, thirdly, let us hear the
testimony of some father of the church that this is the very meaning of
the gospel. St. Augustine, in the book of questions of the New and of
the Old Testament,[21] in the seventy-fifth question says in this manner:
"The payment of this money was head money paid for the heads." And
after follows: "When our Savior commanded this double tribute to be
paid for Himself and for Peter, in so commanding He satisfied [the
tax for] all the rest of the apostles, for they all were contained in Him
because He was their master. And as they all were contained in our
Savior, so after our Savior they all were contained in Peter. For Christ
made him the head of them all." Here note from St. Augustine that
St. Peter, because he was head of them all and they all were contained in

---

18. A silver coin worth two drachmas, or half a shekel.

19. Matt. 17:24–27.

20. I.e., without a master.

21. St. Augustine of Hippo (354–430). Fisher may be referring to his *Questions on the Gospels*.

him, therefore this tribute that was paid for him was paid for them all. But yet by another scripture that I enumerated before, St. Augustine proved that all the other apostles were contained in St. Peter: "Simon, Simon, lo Satan has coveted to sift you as a man sifts wheat, but I have prayed for you that your faith shall not fail, and you, once converted to the stable way, confirm your brethren."[22] Upon which words St. Augustine says that Christ did not pray for James and John and for the others, but He prayed for St. Peter in whom the rest were contained.

Consider now how each of these testimonies confirms and strengthens each other. First, the figure and shadow of the old law. Second, the testimony of the Gospels answering the same. And here I bring but one church doctor, whose testimony in the balance of any true Christian man's heart should I think weigh down Martin Luther. But St. Ambrose[23] speaking of didrachmas calls it also "head money." And of St. Peter he says: "Peter is called *petra*[24] because he, first among the gentiles, established the grounds of our faith and, as a stone not easy to be removed, he contained within himself and held all the advantage and greatness of the works of Christ." And St. Gregory says: "Peter is the chief member of the universal church. Paul, Andrew, and John—what else are they but heads of certain and singular peoples?" Whereby it appears that while they were chiefs of every one of the peoples that they had cure of,[25] St. Peter was chief of the universal church. St. Jerome[26] also says, speaking of Peter: "Peter was one chosen out among twelve, to the intent that he, being made their head, should take away all occasions of schismatic division." St. Cyprian[27] furthermore says, speaking of Peter when he confessed Christ Jesus to be the Son of God: "There spoke Peter, upon whom

---

22. Luke 22:31.
23. St. Ambrose (c. 330–397) was archbishop of Milan and a doctor of the church.
24. "Rock" in Latin.
25. I.e., that they served as ministers and religious guides.
26. St. Jerome (c. 347–420) was a doctor of the church most famous for his translation of the Bible into Latin, a version (known as the Vulgate) that became the standard Bible for western Christendom until the Reformation era.
27. St. Cyprian (c. 200–258) was a leading North African theologian.

the church was to be built." But how should the church be built upon
him if he were not the head and chief member of the church?

All these are holy fathers of the Latin Church,[28] all men of great
learning, all men of singular holiness whose virtuous living has been
confirmed by miracles done both in their lives and after their deaths.
Likewise among the Greeks.[29] Chrysostom,[30] after he had praised St.
Paul, speaks of St. Peter, saying that St. Peter, who "was the head of
the apostles," was thus such another. And often he called St. Peter "the
chief of the apostles and the mouth of the disciples, and the top and
head of all the college." And Origen[31] says: "See what was said of our
Lord to that great fundament of the church and most stable stone [i.e.,
Peter]. O man of little faith, why did you doubt?"

If all these many testimonies, both of Greeks and Latins, shall
not counterpoise against one friar, what reason is this? I trust there
is no true Christian man who will not be moved by the testimony of
all these, especially when they are grounded in so plain and evident a
figure of the old law, and in so clear a light of the holy Gospels.

But here Luther will say that he cannot conceive of two high priests.
Of this I marvel greatly since it is manifest that Aaron was called "high"
in Scripture, and if he were high priest and Moses was no whit beneath
him, then they must both of them be high, one of them under another,
in comparison to other people. So as St. Paul makes many heads, saying: "See here there are three heads for a woman: God, Christ, and
her husband."[32] And yet besides all these she has a head of her own. It
would be a monstrous sight to see a woman without a head, whatever
comfort her husband should have for her. So then a woman, notwithstanding that she has a head of her own to govern her according to the
will and pleasure of her husband, yet she also has her husband to be
her head, and Christ to be her head, and God to be her head. How

---

28. I.e., the Roman Catholic Church.

29. I.e., members of the Christian church of the Eastern Roman Empire (or
Byzantium), also known as the Orthodox Church.

30. John Chrysostom (c. 347–407), a church father.

31. Origen (c. 184–c. 153) was a church father and theologian active in
Alexandria.

32. 1 Cor. 11:3; Eph. 5:23.

much more our holy mother church, which is the spouse of Christ, has a head of her own, that is to say the pope, and yet nevertheless Christ Jesus her husband is her head, and almighty God is her head also.

But now let us return to our instruction. Thus then you understand how in the universal church of Christ the Spirit of Truth remains forever, and the head of this church, the pope, is under Christ. By this then it may appear that the Spirit of Christ is not in Martin Luther. The spirit of every natural body gives life no further than to the members and parts of the same body that are naturally joined to the head; and so it must be likewise in the mystical body of our holy mother church.

For as much as this wretched man has divided himself from the head of this body, which is the vicar of Christ, how can he have within him the Spirit of this body, which is the Spirit of Truth? And especially when he has divided himself with such pride, arrogance, and presumption, which is most odious to this Holy Spirit, and has so contemptuously, so presumptuously, so maliciously condemned, set to nothing, and all too outraged the head of Christ's church, to whom, as to his chief spiritual father, by reason of his religion he has vowed and promised obedience.[33] How can this man have in him the Spirit of God, this Holy Spirit of Truth? And here I make an end to the first instruction.

The Second Instruction

Here follows the second instruction against the pernicious doctrine of Martin Luther.

For the second instruction the following words answer: "And He shall bear witness or give evidence of Me."[34] What marvelous power, what wonderful operation the beams of the sun have, which, as we see this time of the year, spread upon the ground and quicken and make many creatures live that before appeared as dead. Whoever viewed and beheld in the winter season the trees when they were withered and

---

33. I.e., because he is an Augustinian friar, he has sworn to obey the church.
34. John 15:26.

their leaves shaken from them, and all the moisture shrunk down to the root, and no delight of greenness or of life appearing outwardly, if he had no experience of this matter before, he would think it an unlikely thing that the same trees should revive again and be so delightfully clad with leaves and flowers as we now see them. And yet this is done by the subtle operation and secret workings of the sunbeams spread upon the ground.

Nevertheless not every beam of the sun has this power. It is a truth that the beams of the sun in winter are light as they are now, this time of the year, but that light is so faint and feeble that it gives no life, for then we would have herbs and trees growing as well in winter as they now do this time of the year. The cause of this weakness is that the sun shows so low near the ground that its beams slant upon the ground and do not rebound nor double back on themselves again toward the sun, and this is the cause of this weakness. You see when a ball is thrown slantingly at a wall, it flies forward and does not rebound backward directly against he who was the thrower. But when it is directly cast against a wall with a great violence, then it does directly rebound again. It is the same with sunbeams: the nearer the sun draws to us now this time of the year, the more directly its beams beat upon the ground and the more directly they rebound and return again toward the sun. And by the reason of the nearness of beam to beam, there arises a greater strength in the beam and a fuller light. For "every power that is gathered together is stronger."[35]

A single thread is not near as strong as a double. Nor is a single beam of sun near as mighty as when it is doubled and twisted in itself by rebounding and reflection. Furthermore, from these two rises a heat, a warmness that is the principal worker of life in every creature. But for all this we are not yet sure that any tree is alive until we see some putting forth of buds or leaves out of the same tree.

This example, if you perceive it, may induce us to conceive how wonderfully the spiritual sun, almighty God, works by the spiritual and invisible beams of His light spread upon the soul of man or upon

---

35. Here Fisher quotes the English natural philosopher Roger Bacon in his study of optics, *Perspectiva* (1267).

the church, both of which are called in Scripture "spiritual earth." "Our Lord shall give His gracious influence and our earth shall yield fruitful works."[36] The beams of almighty God spread upon our souls, quickening them and causing this life in us and the fruit of good works. First they cause the light of faith, but this is a very slender light without the rebounding of hope and the heat of charity.[37] Faith without hope is a slender beam and of little power. But join to it hope that rebounds up to God again, "to things which are not seen,"[38] and then it is much stronger than it was before. For now this is doubled and twisted in itself and gathered nearer to Him and made more valiant and mighty than it was before. Before it was like the faith that St. Peter had when Christ bade him come to Him upon the sea; he believed his master but he had no very firm hope that he might walk there; he was not strong in his faith and therefore our Savior said unto him: "O you of little faith, why did you doubt?"[39] But of the strong faith that has a confidence and hope joined to it, He says in another place: "If you had faith like that of a grain of mustard seed, you should command this mountain to remove itself and it should, by your faith, move away."[40] This is a great faith and has also confidence and hope adjoined to it. A grain of mustard seed is very little, but it has a great power joined together and gathered within it. So when the beams of faith and hope are joined together in one point then it is of mighty power. The beams of the sun, when they are gathered together by reflection of a burning glass, are so mighty that they will set tinder or cloth on fire. And it is likewise with beams of faith and hope when they are jointly joined

---

36. Ps. 85:12.

37. Here Fisher, as with Eck, criticizes Luther's idea of *sola fide* by drawing on the popular understanding that faith alone is cold and dead, and requires hope and love (or charity) to perfect it and make it salvific. See 1 Cor. 13, and especially 1 Cor. 13:2 (which Fisher quotes below): "And if I have prophetic powers, and understand all mysteries and all knowledge, and if I have all faith, so as to remove mountains, but do not have love, I am nothing."

38. 2 Cor. 4:18. "Because we look not at what can be seen but at what cannot be seen; for what can be seen is temporary, but what cannot be seen is eternal."

39. Matt. 14:31.

40. Matt. 17:20.

together and united together. If a man had such a faith and confidence, then he might command a great mountain to remove for his pleasure and this would be a mighty faith. Nevertheless, if a man had such a faith, but lacked the heat of charity, he would be as a dead tree. For St. Paul says: "though I have all faith, so that I could remove mountains, and have not charity, I am nothing."[41] If I have all faith, He who speaks of all leaves none unspoken of. If I have all faith, and so mighty a faith that by my faith I may remove at my commandment great mountains, yet if I lack the heat of charity, I am nothing but a dead trunk of a tree without life. And therefore St. James says: "Faith without the fruit of good works is dead."[42] For this reason our instruction says: "He shall bear witness of Me."[43] Of whom? Of Christ. What is Christ? "The true light, which enlightens every creature coming into this world."[44] Who shall bear witness or give evidence of this light? The Spirit of God. "The heat of charity of God is spread in our hearts by the Holy Spirit which is given unto us."[45] Heat of charity gives evidence that that light is living. No matter how much light of faith a man has, unless he also has this heat of charity steering his soul and bringing forth living works, he is but a dead trunk and as a tree without life. For as I said, even if the natural sun shines ever so bright upon a tree, if this tree has in it no greenness nor putting forth of buds and leaves, this tree is not alive. So when the beams of the spiritual sun are spread upon our souls, if we do not feel the steering heat of fruitful works, our souls are simply dead.

But now what purpose does this instruction serve? That it subverts one great ground of Martin Luther, which is this: that faith alone without works justifies a sinner. Upon this ground he builds many other erroneous articles, and especially that the sacraments of Christ's church do not justify; but only faith. This is a perilous article able to subvert all the order of the church. But touching these sacraments,

---

41. 1 Cor. 13:2.

42. James 2:26. For this reason Luther considered the Epistle of James "a book of straw."

43. John 15:26.

44. John 1:9.

45. Rom. 5:5.

the king's grace,[46] our sovereign lord, in his own person has with his pen so substantially fought against Martin Luther that I do not doubt that every true Christian man who shall read his book[47] shall see those blessed sacraments cleared and delivered from the scandalous mouth and cruel teeth that Martin Luther has set upon them, wherein all England may take great comfort and especially all those who love learning. Plato says: "Commonwealths shall be blessed when either those who are philosophers govern, or else those who govern give themselves to philosophy."[48] And Scripture exhorts princes to the same saying: "And now you who are kings, study to have understanding, and you who take upon yourselves the judgments of the world, endeavor to have learning."[49]

But now let us return to our matter again. For this ground Luther brings in St. Paul saying in diverse places that a man is justified by his faith only, without works. Nevertheless, St. Augustine says that St. Paul's words were misunderstood in the beginning of the church, which, as he says, is why the other apostles stressed the contrary in their epistles. But some here think that Martin Luther has little regard for St. Augustine. And this is true, yet it is a foul presumption. Let him at least believe the other apostles whom without manifest heresy he cannot deny. St. James says: "A man is justified by his deeds and not by his faith alone."[50] Such things St. James not only says, but also proves by diverse ways. One is this: "The devils also believe, and tremble."[51] The devils have faith, and yet no man may say that the devils are justified by their faith. How many who live in horrible sin still have the faith of Christ Jesus, and would rather die than deny their faith? But for all that they are not justified. But if only faith justified both, they and the devils would also be justified.

---

46. The English king, Henry VIII Tudor (1491–1547).

47. Fisher is referring here to Henry VIII's 1521 treatise, *Defense of the Seven Sacraments*, which would be widely read and published in numerous editions.

48. Plato, *The Republic*, Book 5, 473c–d.

49. Ps. 2:10.

50. James 2:24.

51. James 2:19. Notice that Eck uses the same citation against Luther.

Second, the same example that St. Paul uses with the Romans to prove that faith justifies a sinner without works, is the one St. James used to the contrary. The example I mean is that of Abraham, which appears in the same place [in James' epistle]. But you will then say: Sir, are these apostles contrary to each other? To this St. Augustine says indeed not, but that St. James only contradicts that which might be misconstrued and mistaken in St. Paul. For St. Paul speaks of the works that go before faith, and St. James speaks of the works that follow after faith. St. Paul means that the work of circumcision, or of other works of the law, was not necessary for justifying Abraham to go before his Father, but his faith without them did justify him.[52] St. James speaks of the fruitful work that follows after faith, which gives evidence of a living faith, and these justify a man. If Abraham had not had this faith, he would not have been justified; if Abraham had not been ready to offer up his son Isaac at the commanding of God, he would not have been justified. But because he was so ready therefore he had faith. "Abraham was justified by his works."[53] Thus St. James speaks not against St. Paul, but against the misunderstanding and misconception of him. St. Peter also speaks of this misconception in his second epistle, saying: "In the epistles of our right dear brother Paul are some things hard to be conceived, which unstable minds misconstrue, just as they do many other Scriptures, to their own damnation."[54] Thus you may see that various others have misconstrued St. Paul before this, as now Martin Luther does, to his own peril and damnation.

But here one thing I marvel greatly about Martin Luther especially, is that he says that in all Scripture there is no more testimony against him but this one place of St. James. Yet it is not to be doubted that many more may be brought forward. And first, our Savior in the Gospel of Luke says: "Give alms and all things shall be clean unto you."[55] What is this cleanness but the justification of

---

52. Rom. 4:2.
53. James 2:21.
54. 2 Pet. 3:16.
55. Luke 11:41.

our souls, which is promised for the works of almsgiving? No matter how much I believe, if I do not relieve the poor in their necessity, I shall not attain this cleanness. Furthermore, in the Gospel of Matthew: "If you do forgive those who have grieved you by their offenses, your Father in heaven shall do likewise to you. And if you do not forgive men who have grieved you by their offenses, nor shall your Father forgive you your offenses done against Him."[56] Additionally he says in the same gospel: "If we work not the will of almighty God the Father, we shall not be justified nor enter into the kingdom of heaven."[57] Besides these, in the same gospel: "Unless your justice or your manner of living is better and more ample than the justice and living of the Jews and Pharisees, you shall not enter into the kingdom of heaven."[58] This is to be understood as the justice of works, as clearly appears in all that follows. Besides this he says: "All who hear my words and do not work toward them are like an unwise man who builds his house upon an unsure ground."[59] And St. Paul also says: "Those who are only hearers of the law of God shall not be justified, but the workers toward it."[60] And St. James says: "Be workers of the word of God, and not only hearers, for then you deceive yourself."[61] And St. Paul again says: "If you live after the works of your flesh you shall die. But if you mortify in you by the Spirit the works of your flesh, you shall live."[62] And finally St. Paul says, concluding his own judgment: "Faith which is wrought by love."[63] In accordance with this, St. James says: "You see how faith helped his works, and how by works his faith was made perfect?"[64] By all these testimonies you may plainly see that not only faith is sufficient, but love and works

---

56. Matt. 6:14–15.
57. Matt. 7:21. "Not everyone who says to Me, 'Lord, Lord,' will enter the kingdom of heaven, but only the one who does the will of My Father in heaven."
58. Matt. 5:20.
59. Matt. 7:26.
60. Rom. 2:13.
61. James 1:22.
62. Rom. 8:13.
63. Gal. 5:6.
64. James 2:22.

are also required for the justifying of our souls. And so much for the second instruction.

The Third Instruction

Here follows the third instruction against Martin Luther.

Touching the third instruction, it follows in the gospel: "You shall bear witness, because you are conversant with Me from the beginning."[65] To whom shall they bear witness, but to the universal church of Christ? Their witness, then, must be allowed of every true Christian man.

Of these words and of the others enumerated above, it shall appear that more testimony must be admitted for sufficient authority than only that which is written in the Bible. If we may establish this one thing, it will cast down a great number of Martin Luther's articles. But for this we must consider these three Persons[66] of whom this gospel has made mention. Though all their works are undivided and not separated from each other, but jointly go together, Scripture assigned these three Persons to three separate times when They have instructed man of the truth necessary for him to believe. First, almighty God the Father instructed our elders by His prophets. As St. Paul says: "Almighty God, the first Person in the godhead, in many diverse ways instructed our fathers by His prophets."[67] By "our fathers" St. Paul means here the Jews, from whom we spiritually descended. For Abraham, who was their carnal father, is also our spiritual father. Now almighty God the Father taught them by His prophets, yet although their prophesies are written in Scripture, yet there were many more things that they said that were unwritten and that were of as great an authority as those that were written. This the Jewish master calls cabala, which is derived from man to man by mouth only, and not by writings.

After this, the second Person, the Son of God, our Savior Christ Jesus, was sent by His Father into this world to instruct man, both by

---

65. John 15:27.
66. I.e., God the Father, Jesus Christ, and the Holy Spirit.
67. Heb. 1:1.

Himself and by His apostles who were conversant with Him (as the gospel says here) from the beginning. These blessed apostles also left to us many things by mouth that are not written in the Bible. This is apparent from St. Paul—who came after them and was not present when Christ said these words to them—in the Second Epistle of Thessalonians: "Be constant and keep those instructions and teachings that you have learned from us either by mouth or else by writing."[68] If St. Paul (who was later than the other apostles, to whom these words were said by Christ) wishes to have his traditions observed and kept, both those that he told them by mouth and those that he wrote with his pen, why should not likewise the traditions of all the other apostles be of similar strength to cause faith and to bear witness of the truth? Here you may see by express Scripture of St. Paul that we are bound to believe many more things than are written and put in the Bible. We shall confirm this by Origen, who is an ancient doctor of the church and to whom in this point great faith should be given. He, in his fifth homily on the Book of Numbers, says: "But in the observances of the church there are many things that are necessary for us to do, and yet the reason why we do so is not open to all men. As an example, when we make our prayers kneeling and when, among all the other places of heaven, we choose the east part toward which we make our prayer, I think that the reasons for these are not easily known to any man. Also, of the observances and rites that we use for the sacrament of the altar to be consecrated, or for the sacrament of baptism to be ministered, who can express the reasons for all those words, gestures, orders, ques-tions, answers, that are customarily used there? And yet nevertheless all these we bear, covered and hid, upon our shoulders when we perform and execute them according to the traditions and teachings that we have received, commended to us by the great bishop Christ and by His children, the holy apostles."[69] From these words of Origen it clearly does appear that many such traditions were left to Christian people by Christ and His apostles, which we must follow notwithstanding that they are not written in Scripture. To which purpose I might also bring

---

68. 2 Thess. 2:15.
69. Origen, *Homilies on Numbers*, Homily 5, Numbers 4:1.4.

the testimony of Damascene,[70] Demose,[71] Augustine, Jerome, and others as well.

Thirdly, the third Person in the Trinity, that is to say the Holy Spirit of Truth, was sent from the other two to abide with us forever, and to be as a continual comforter in Christ's church when the storms and tempests of heresy arise and against all faltering doubtfulness, to teach us the very certain truth upon which we should rest. After the apostles departed from us, the Holy Spirit did and does remain and shall remain with us until the world's end. But by whom, I pray you, does He speak to us? By whom does He teach us any truth? By whom else but by the fathers and doctors of the church. By their mouths this Holy Spirit teaches us every truth. "It is not you who speaks, but the Holy Spirit of your Father which speaks within you."[72] When St. Basil was baptized, a wonderful light was seen about him which was, without doubt, a sensible token of the Holy Ghost. And likewise, while St. Ambrose was writing about the Forty-third Psalm,[73] a light was seen above his head in a manner of a shield, which little by little entered into his mouth in a very token of the Spirit of God. And so likewise it was of the others. For this reason it is not to be doubted that the Holy Ghost speaks in such holy bishops and doctors of the church. But this is much more so in councils, when many of them were assembled together. Forever as the storms and tempests of heresies arose, so they were at length suppressed and overpowered by this Holy Spirit speaking in the mouths of the fathers and doctors of the church, and sometime by general councils and assemblies of many bishops together.

In the Council of Nicaea[74] were 309 bishops in whom the Holy Ghost spoke to confute a heresy that then sore troubled the church.

---

70. St. John of Damascus (c. 645–749), a doctor of the church.

71. Unclear who Fisher is referring to here.

72. Matt. 10:20.

73. Ambrose's *Explanation of the Psalms*.

74. The First Council of Nicaea was called by the Roman emperor Constantine I in 325, and dealt with the problem of the Arian heresy.

After that, in the Council of Constantinople,[75] 150 bishops assembled, and in them the Holy Ghost spoke to the destruction of another heresy that then arose in the church. In the council held in Ephesus,[76] in a great city of Asia so named, were assembled 300 bishops in whom then the Holy Spirit spoke, to the confounding of another heresy that was aloft. And so continually, from time to time, ever as these clouds arose and made any great tempests and began to lighten and show a false light of misconstruing of Scripture, this Holy Spirit was ready by these fathers to inform the universal church of the certain truth.

So then I say that we have to confirm those things that are taught us by the church. First, the prophets who were instructed by the Father almighty God, and also their cabala, that is to say their secret teachings not written in the Bible. Second, the apostles, who were instructed by our Savior Christ Jesus, and also their traditions not written in the Bible. Third, the holy fathers and doctors of the church who were informed by the Holy Spirit of Truth, both in their expositions of Scripture and by the general assemblies and councils they have had up to now.

If there were a fourth Person in the trinity, or another Spirit to be sent unto us from almighty God, we might yet be in some doubt whether Martin Luther had met with this Spirit along the way and taken Him from us. But since we are assured that there are no more than three Persons in the godhead of whom this gospel makes mention, and that every one of them has done His diligence to instruct us of the truth, and furthermore that there is no other Holy Spirit but this Spirit of Truth, and He also shall abide with us forever and ascertain us of every truth, then we may be sure that Martin Luther does not have this Spirit when he teaches us against the truth that has been taught us by this Spirit. For he cuts away the traditions of the apostles, and refutes the general councils, and condemns the doctrine of the holy fathers and doctors of the church, and labors to subvert all

---

75. The First Council of Constantinople was called by the Roman emperor Theodosius I in 381, and dealt again with the problem of the Arian heresy and other challenges to church doctrine, including Apollinarism.

76. The First Council of Ephesus was called by the Roman emperor Theodosius II in 431, and dealt with heresies such as Nestorianism.

the ordinances of the church, and namely the seven sacraments, and takes away the freedom of man's will, and affirms that all things happen by necessity, contrary to all the doctrine of Christ's church. We may be sure, therefore, that he has some other wretched spirit, some spirit of error and not the Spirit of Truth. St. Paul says: "In the latter days of the church, some shall go from the true faith of Christ's church and give heed to the spirits of error and to the teaching of the devil."[77] And here note the words "shall go." For St. Paul says in another place: "There shall be a falling away first."[78] That is to say, before the coming of the Antichrist there shall be a notable dispersal and departing from the faith of the church. And it is not unlikely for this to occur at this very time through the efforts of this most perilous heretic.

Here Martin Luther with his shrewd brain will wrestle against us. He will say that the councils sometimes err, and that the doctors very often disagree. And as they err and disagree at one time or in one place, so maybe they do in another, and therefore he says he is bound to believe none of them at all. To this may be answered that this is not reasonable, even if it shall well appear so. The prophets, left to themselves, sometimes strayed from the truth. "The Spirit of prophecy does not always shine bright upon the minds of the prophets."[79] As an example, King David, intending to build the temple to almighty God, met with the prophet Nathan, asking whether he should carry out his intent or not. And the prophet Nathan told him to take it in hand and to do all that he intended within his heart to do. "Do all that you intend in your heart, for our Lord God is with you."[80] Yet he was mistaken; it was not as he said. Shall we now, for this mistake, trust none of the other things that this prophet Nathan said besides this? God forbid! Likewise of the apostle St. Peter, when he said to Christ: "You are Christ, the Son of the living God."[81] He spoke this by revelation, and here our Savior

---

77. 1 Tim. 4:1.

78. 2 Thess. 2:3.

79. A quote from Pope Gregory I (c. 540–604).

80. 2 Sam. 7:3.

81. Matt. 16:16.

praised him and said: "You are blessed Peter, the son of Jonah."[82] But a little later he tried to dissuade our Savior from His passion and said: "Not so, good Lord,"[83] and in this he spoke wrongly. Shall we now, because he spoke wrongly this second time, not believe his first statement? That would not be reasonable.

Almighty God also allowed the prophets and the apostles sometime to err, to the intent that we might know they were only humans. And when they spoke truth, then they had this from God, and when they spoke otherwise than truth, then this came from themselves. And so likewise I say of the doctors. Though they sometimes erred—because then we might know that they were humans and that they had been left to themselves—we shall not therefore deny them generally. And the councils also, though some of the latest councils— which perhaps were not gathered in that meekness and charity that was expedient (something I will not affirm)—were permitted to go amiss in some articles, should we therefore damn all the remaining ones? It would be unreasonable. And this may suffice for the third instruction.

The Fourth Instruction

Here follows the fourth instruction.

The fourth and final instruction takes away the defense that may be laid for Martin Luther by his adherents, which defense also may soon overthrow weak souls when they shall hear it. Their defense consists of three points. First they say that Martin Luther is a man deeply learned in the Scriptures, grounding all his opinions upon them; a man of religious life; and someone who has many adherents because of his learning and virtue. Second they say that he has a mind fixed on God, and allows no man's authority to bar him from speaking the truth, so much so that he has excommunicated the pope, as he thinks in his own conscience that those who do not follow his doctrine are not part of the Catholic Church. Third, he has a marvelously fervent zeal for God,

82. Matt. 16:17.
83. Matt. 16:22.

for which he labors to convert all the world to his opinion, thinking assuredly that he thereby offers God a special sacrifice and pleasure.

When a weak soul hears this, he is in immediate peril of giving faith to it and mistrusting the doctrine of the church. For who may not think such a man is on the right path? But on this account the rest of the gospel that follows answers clearly: "This I have told you before, to the intent that you shall not quail in your faith, for they shall divide you from their synagogues and the time shall come that every man that murders you shall think that he thereby does great service unto God."[84] These words may be taught by some to pertain only to the time of the Jews, who expelled the apostles from their synagogues, or to the time of the tyrants, who slew many Christian people in the beginning of the church. But if that were true, then these words would not be a general instruction for the universal church, something we argued against Luther at the beginning of our sermon. Therefore, these words pertain instead to the time of the heretics. First, because this persecution continued longer than the other two, for the persecution by the Jews was soon set aside, and the persecution by the tyrants ran its course in a season. But the heretics have persecuted the church from the ascension of Christ and shall do so until the coming of the Antichrist. Furthermore, the persecution by the heretics is and was much more perilous, for the Jews and the tyrants were manifest enemies of Christ and abhorred His Scriptures, but these heretics pretend a special favor toward Christ, and color all their heresies with His Scriptures. The Jews and the tyrants, when they had slain the bodies of Christian men, still sent their souls to everlasting glory; but the heretics, by misconstruing the Scriptures of God through their false doctrine and erroneous opinions and pestilent heresies, slay the souls of Christian people and send them to everlasting damnation. Therefore these words must instead be understood as referring to the persecution that was made by the heretics.

Now then Christian man, when you hear that Martin Luther is a man of great learning, and has great expertise in the Scriptures, and is reputed for virtuous living, and has many great adherents, think that

---

84. John 16:1–2.

many such men have come before him in the church of Christ who, by their learning and misinterpretation of Scripture, have caused tempests in the church before this time. . . .

And every one of these heretics grounded his heresy upon Scripture. And many of them were men of strong intelligence, of deep learning, of mighty reason, and of pretended virtue, and had the proper faith to turn and twist the Scriptures, to make them apparent for their erroneous opinions. Finally, their life, learning, and handling of Scripture were such that they had many great adherents and supporters, both among bishops and among emperors and other Christian princes as well, who were misled by them.

Therefore it was necessary that our Savior Christ Jesus, because of the great inestimable goodness and the tender love that He bears for His church, should leave instruction and warning to all Christian people and to His universal church about this persecution. And so He did, saying: "I have told you these things before, so you shall not quail in your faith."[85] What has He told us before? This: that the Spirit of Truth shall remain in the church forever, and that in all such storms and tempests He shall be a comforter to us. O Christian man, hear this gracious warning of our Savior Christ! Mark well what He says! I have warned you, He says, of these things before, so when they occur you shall not be overthrown in your souls by them. It is as though He said: "When you see the storms arise, when you behold the thick black clouds aloft that darken all the face of the heavens, shadow from you the clear light of the sun, and show a false glistering light that issues from the cloud and from the spirit of the tempest, and you hear the terrible threatening of their thundering, then be constant in your faith; believe with a living faith as does your mother, the holy church, and put your trust in the Spirit of Truth, who shall be your comforter until the world's end."

Furthermore, when you hear, Christian man, that Martin Luther has a mind fixed on God and allows no man's authority to bar him from speaking the truth, and argues that all those who do not follow his doctrine are divided from the Catholic Church, so much so that he has excommunicated the pope—O wonderful presumption!

---

85. John 16:1.

O intolerable madness!—then know this for certain, that all the other heretics did likewise. They argued that they themselves and their adherents alone were of the Catholic Church, and reckoned that all others who did not follow their opinion were divided from the church. . . .

Nevertheless the church of Christ is but one: one, holy, catholic, and apostolic. This church is one, having one head, the pope, who is the vicar of Christ, because of whom it is called "one." And although there are many sinners in this church, yet because of the holy sacraments that renew and repair sinners daily, and because of the Holy Spirit who continually remains within it, it is called "holy." And because it is not limited to any one nation, but is in common to all nations, therefore it is called "catholic," that is to say universal. And finally, because it is derived from the apostles and especially from the prince of the apostles, St. Peter, therefore it is called "apostolic." Only this church is the spouse of Christ. All others that resemble it are not of this church, but are synagogues of Satan and councils of the devil. And therefore, Christian man, do not be astonished that they excommunicate and divide true Christians from their synagogues. For our Savior has given us warning of this before, saying, as it follows in the gospel: "They shall excommunicate you and divide you from their synagogues."[86]

Thirdly, Christian man, when you hear that Martin Luther has so great a zeal for God and thinks in his conscience that he is bound to do as he does, and thinks in so doing that he pleases God and does a special service to God and recommits to almighty God all the souls that by his false doctrine he actually slays and murders, yet nevertheless be strong in your faith and see that in this point our Savior has also warned the church, saying: "The time comes when every man that murders you shall think that he does acceptable service to God."[87] . . .

Conclusion

Now then, here I make an end. I have informed you, according to my promise, of four instructions that are graciously offered to us by

86. John 16:2.
87. John 16:2.

this gospel. First, that the Holy Spirit, who is the third Person in the Divinity, was sent from the Father almighty God, and from His Son, our Savior Christ Jesus, to be the Spirit of Truth, residing forever in the church of Christ, and to be as a comforter from time to time against all storms and tempests of heresies, establishing for us in the time of every doubtfulness the very truth that we shall hold onto and that shall keep us. By this instruction I showed three things. First, that this instruction and the whole gospel pertains to the universal church of Christ, which I proved by Luther's own words. Second, that the head of this universal church is the pope under Christ, a point that takes away one great ground of Martin Luther and severely shakes many of his erroneous articles. Third, that Martin Luther, by dividing himself from the head of this body, cannot have in him this Spirit of Truth.

For the second instruction I showed that the heat of charity, spread in our hearts by the Holy Spirit of God, gives evidence of the living light of faith, shining upon our souls from our Savior Christ. By this instruction another great ground of Martin Luther was undermined, which is that only faith justifies a sinner, without works.

For the third instruction I showed that the teachings left to the church by the holy apostles contain testimony for us of the faith of Christ, and of what things we should believe in His church; thereby dissolving another ground of Martin Luther, who will not admit any other testimony but that which is written in Scripture. Against him I proved that besides the written Scriptures, he must also receive the unwritten traditions of the apostles, and in addition the general councils in which the Holy Ghost spoke, and the interpretations of Scriptures made by the holy bishops and doctors of the church, by whose mouths the third Person in the godhead, the Spirit of Truth, spoke and speaks, informing the church for this time just as the Father almighty God did by His prophets before, and as did His Son, the second Person, by His apostles.

For the fourth instruction I showed you that the defense that is made for Martin Luther by his adherents, whereby many weak souls are overthrown, is clearly taken away by the most loving and most gracious forewarning of our Savior Christ, as you have heard in the end of the gospel. And yet soon after, out of His most excellent charity, He warned all His Christian people, saying and repeating: "These things I have told you to the intent that when the dangers shall befall, yet you may remember that I previously did warn you of them."[88] Whoever is thus often warned but will still give faith to Martin Luther, or to any other such heretic, rather than to Christ Jesus and to the Spirit of Truth who remains in the church of Christ until the world's end especially to inform us of the truth, is a man who goes far wide from the straight way. He is never likely to enter into the port of everlasting rest that we all desire and long to enter, and into which He brings us "who, with the Father and the Holy Ghost, livest and reignest God, world without end."[89] Amen.

---

88. John 16:4.
89. Part of the prayer said during the Mass.

IV. Thomas Müntzer and the Peasants' War

Introduction

Thomas Müntzer (c. 1490–1525) was a talented biblical and literary scholar and clergyman who became an early supporter of Martin Luther's reforming ideas. In 1520 he was appointed pastor in Zwickau in Thuringia (a region within Saxony), most likely thanks to a recommendation from Luther. Müntzer's ideas were too radical for local officials, however, and he was soon expelled from his post. He then fled to Bohemia, where he hoped to find a more sympathetic congregation among the followers of the fifteenth-century reformer and martyred heretic Jan Hus. Given an initial warm welcome, here too Müntzer soon met opposition, and after a period of uncertainty and frequent displacement he finally returned to Saxony. There he settled in the small town of Allstedt, where he was named a pastor in 1523 and where he attempted to create a new godly community guided by the Holy Spirit and based on the principle of communal responsibility. From Allstedt he also preached his famous July 1524 *Sermon to the Princes*, in which he painted himself as a new Daniel, warned of the imminent apocalypse, and demanded support for the Reformation from Duke John of Saxony (the brother of the elector) and his son. His appeals were met with hostility, and in August he was once again forced to flee his post. This humiliating departure was no doubt facilitated by a stinging tirade lobbed against him by Martin Luther (*Letter to the Princes of Saxony*),[1] for although the two men had been close years before, Müntzer's ideas had long since morphed into something unrecognizable to Luther, and they were now bitter enemies.

---

1. *Letter to the Princes of Saxony against the Rebellious Spirit at Allstedt* (July 1524). This was probably directed not just at Müntzer but also at Andreas Karlstadt, a former colleague of Luther.

Thomas Müntzer, by Christoffel van Sichem, 1608.

Luther taught that Scripture was the sole source of divine truth, but Müntzer, strongly influenced by his earlier studies of German mystics and, while at Zwickau, by the reformer Nikolaus Storch (a member of the so-called Zwickau Prophets), had become convinced that God still speaks to humanity, and that Christians should look beyond the Bible and accept the unmediated inspiration of the Holy Spirit or inner light of God. Luther, he argued, was too intent on the literal words of the Bible, wielding it as a "paper pope" and rejecting the internal experience of the Spirit in favor of the dry scholarship of textual analysis. The most important thing, Müntzer wrote in his 1521 *Prague Manifesto*, was that one open oneself up to God, for "when the seed falls on the good field, that is, in hearts full of the fear of God, then they become the paper or parchment upon which God writes the real Holy Scripture with His living finger, not with ink."[2] For Luther, however, such an idea was dangerous. The Holy Spirit guided us to the true meaning of Scripture, he argued, and any attempt to separate the Spirit from

---

2. Peter Matheson, ed. and trans., *The Collected Works of Thomas Müntzer* (Edinburgh: T & T Clark, 1988), 365.

the gospel would lead only to misunderstanding and corruption. "It must be firmly maintained," he explained much later, "that God gives no one His Spirit or grace apart from the external Word which goes before. We say this to protect ourselves from the enthusiasts, that is, the 'spirits,' who boast that they have the Spirit apart from and before contact with the Word. On this basis, they judge, interpret, and twist the Scripture or oral Word according to their pleasure . . . [and] set themselves up as shrewd judges between the Spirit and the letter without knowing what they say or teach."[3]

Another important distinction between Luther and Müntzer was their understanding of justification and the relationship between grace (or the unmerited mercy and love of God) and the law (or the commandments of God). Luther taught that humans are justified by faith alone through God's grace, not by works of the law; Christ fulfilled the law for humanity and atoned for its sins, and so the law was now superseded. Müntzer, however, argued that humans needed to be Christ's disciples, to imitate Him and participate spiritually in His suffering, and also to fulfill the law. So while Luther argued that the law shows people their utter unworthiness, sinfulness, and dependence on faith as a gift from God and as their sole path to salvation (see Freedom, §9), Müntzer argued that the law shows people their lack of belief, which can only be converted to belief by the chastisement of the Holy Spirit working within the believer. Thus works were required in addition to faith, a philosophy that provides for some concept of free will. Luther, however, saw Müntzer's focus on the internal word of God as encouraging dangerous demagoguery and radicalism. He famously criticized a similar view in his former friend, Andreas Karlstadt, scoffing that he had "swallowed the Holy Spirit feathers and all."[4]

Müntzer and Luther also had very different conceptions of the proper process of reform and of the nature of the Christian community. While the Catholic Church and men such as Eck saw Luther as a

---

3. From Luther's *Schmalcald Articles* (1537), in Robert Kolb and Timothy J. Wenger, eds., *The Book of Concord: the Confessions of the Evangelical Lutheran Church* (Minneapolis, Fortress Press, 2000), 322.

4. Martin Luther, *D. Martin Luthers Werke: Kritische Gesamtausgabe*, vol. 18 (Weimar: H. Böhlau, 1908), 66:19–20.

radical, to Müntzer the reform efforts of Luther (or "Father Pussyfoot," as Müntzer called him) were far too weak, hesitant, and gradual. Necessary instead was a more far-reaching and thoroughgoing reform of Christendom that would ready the world for the reign of the Holy Spirit and the imminent end of days. Influenced by his extensive pastoral work with the lower classes, and especially miners, and by the hostility of the Saxon princes to his message, by late 1524 Müntzer had become convinced that the true church could only be restored by the common man, who would, as an instrument of God, lead the inevitable overthrow of all rapacious and unchristian secular rulers. Ecclesiastical and secular authorities could support and further this work, or they would be swept aside. In his *Highly Provoked Defense* of that year, written in direct response to Luther's *Letter to the Princes of Saxony*, Müntzer was thus bitterly critical of Luther's discomfort with any alteration of the contemporary hierarchical class society and his unconditional support for the power of the princes. This was, Müntzer argued, a clear sign that Luther was a pure hypocrite, greedy for honors and preferences and willing to prostitute his theology to win the support of the German nobility.

After his flight from Allstedt, Müntzer ended up in nearby Mühlhausen, where he was named pastor. There his political, social, and economic egalitarianism, along with his apocalyptic desire to cleanse the world of unbelievers before the last days (and by violence if necessary), would soon push him into supporting and then becoming one of the leaders of a large peasant revolt later known as the German Peasants' War (1524–1526). Despite its name, this war was not a single conflict, but a series of connected or related popular uprisings that began in 1524, spread like wildfire throughout central Europe, and culminated in a series of battles in May 1525. And just as local conditions differed, so too did the underlying factors driving this war, although one can make some generalizations about the three issues that seem most consequential. First was the enormous pent-up anger over new and ancient feudal dues, rents, and compulsory labor due from the peasantry to the local nobility and territorial princes. The cost of these extractions could amount to a large portion of a family's income, and did not include the traditional tithes also due to the church. The economic pressure resulting from

such fees and taxes was further exacerbated by inflation and the growing rural population, which meant smaller plot sizes for the peasantry,
lower wages for workers, and a large increase in the number of landless
poor. Second was the frustration and fear caused by the efforts of territorial German princes to strengthen their control over their states. As part
of a larger continent-wide trend, rulers in central Europe had recently
begun to curtail the legal and political autonomy traditionally practiced
by village and town councils within their borders, and even to introduce
the hierarchy-friendly Roman law in place of more egalitarian common
systems of law. Third was the Reformation.

While there has been recent movement among scholars to down-
play the idea that the Reformation caused this rebellion of the common man, it seems clear that the reformers' religious ideas at least
gave the peasants a new theoretical and religious framework for their
grievances.[5] Thus in addition to economic and political demands that
mirrored those issued during earlier uprisings, many peasant demands
of 1524 and 1525 added purely religious articles reflecting the reform
ideas of the time. One of the most famous of these peasant manifes-
tos is *The Twelve Articles*, a document issued by representatives of the
peasants of Upper Swabia in March 1525 and then republished and
disseminated widely. Of the twelve articles listed, nine were almost
exclusively or primarily economic or political. These included demands
for reductions in various taxes and forced labor, for the end to the
nobility's special and exclusive rights over game and forest products,
and for the return of seized common lands. The remaining articles
and the introduction strongly reflected the influence of the Reformation. The very first article, for example, was a demand that the people
have the right to choose and dismiss their own ministers and that the
ministers should preach the gospel "without any additional human
doctrine or commandments"[6]—an idea that had been firmly espoused

---

5. For more on the relationship between the war and the Reformation, see
Peter Blickle, *The Revolution of 1525: The German Peasants' War from a New
Perspective* (Baltimore, 1981); Michael G. Baylor, *The German Reformation and
the Peasants' War: A Brief History with Documents* (Boston: Bedford/St. Martin,
2012), 10–32.

6. Michael G. Baylor, *The Radical Reformation* (Cambridge, 1991), 231–38.

by Martin Luther himself—while the last article expressed the peasants' willingness to be schooled or corrected in their demands based
on Holy Scripture alone (a concept prevalent throughout the document). The third article, with its call for the end of serfdom, also
strongly indicates the influence of Luther and other reformers' idea
of spiritual equality. "Until now," the peasants wrote, "it has been the
custom for us to be regarded as a lord's personal property, which is
deplorable since Christ redeemed us all with the shedding of His precious blood—the shepherd as well as the most highly placed, without
exception. Thus, Scripture establishes that we are and will be free."[7]

Throughout *The Twelve Articles* the peasants thus clearly made use
of Luther, Ulrich Zwingli, and other reformers' stress on the gospel as
the source of truth and basis for spiritual practices. It was then only a
small step, and one taken explicitly by the peasants and radical reformers such as Müntzer, to insist that all social, political, and even economic
practices also be based on godly law and the authority of Scripture. Of
course, Scripture could be used to justify rebellion as well. Luther himself, after all, had based his revolt against the pope and the emperor on
the Bible! At Mühlhausen, Müntzer and his followers thus used the
example of the ancient apostolic church as justification for overthrow-
ing the city council, creating a communistic community of goods, and
readying a peasant army. Müntzer then urged his former parishioners at
Allstedt and others to join the rebellion and to strike down all unbelievers who stood in their way. "Pay no attention to the cries of the godless,"
he insisted. "They will entreat you ever so warmly, they will whimper
and wheedle like children. Show no pity. . . . You must go to it, go to it,
go to it! . . . Don't let your sword grow cold. . . . As long as they live it is
impossible for you to rid yourselves of the fear of men."[8]

Luther agreed that the peasants had indeed been systematically
oppressed and fleeced, but this uprising violated his sense that the
existing social hierarchy must be preserved. In his April 1525 *Admonition to Peace*, therefore, he acknowledged the validity of the peasants' grievances and chided the princes for bringing this trouble on

---

7. Ibid.
8. Mattheson, *Collected Works*, 141–42.

themselves, but firmly rebutted the peasants' use of Scripture to support violence. Only a month later, however, outraged by the extent of the rebellion and horrified by the brutal murders of noblemen and churchmen, Luther penned a further response. This pamphlet, which he titled *Against the Rioting Peasants* (but which was probably given the snappier title *Against the Robbing and Murdering Hordes of Peasants* by his publishers) was a harsh and uncompromising attack on the rebels, and one that repudiated his earlier argument that the gospel should never be defended by force or through bloodshed. The peasants, he wrote, were disloyal, criminal, blasphemous, and anti-Christian; the princes should thus strike without mercy and cut them down like dogs. The peasants' violence and rejection of the godly requirement to obey authority were bad enough, he wrote, but it was even worse that "they cloak such terrible, horrible sin with the gospel" and "call themselves Christian brethren." Their insistence that "all things were created free and in common, and that we have all alike been baptized" was also criminally misguided, for "baptism does not make one free in body and possessions, but in soul; and the gospel does not make

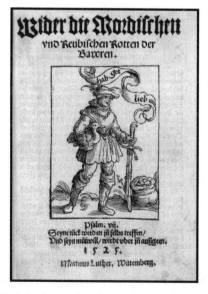

Frontispiece from Martin Luther, *Against the Murdering and Robbing Hordes of Peasants*, 1525.

possessions common."⁹ Luther's message of Christian spiritual freedom, in other words, had been radically transformed into advocacy for
social and political freedom as well.

By June 1525 the majority of the peasant forces had been routed by
the better armed and organized noble armies, though some few fought
on into the following year. Among those defeated was Müntzer, whose
small army was massacred at the battle of Frankenhausen on 15 May
1525, and who was taken prisoner, tortured, and forced to recant and
accept the Catholic Mass before being executed. The rebellion and the
peasant movement failed, and the rebels were treated without mercy.
Luther's *Against the Rioting Peasants* was seen by some as a shocking
betrayal of the common man, while others judged it a hypocritical
attempt to abandon what Luther knew was a losing cause, or to curry
favor with the princes who might help further his Reformation. Faced
with such criticism, he felt compelled to publish an explanation for his
harshness a few months later. Yet even here he continued to justify the
use of violence against rebels, tempering this only with an admonish-
ment of the princes for their brutality and retaliatory excesses.

Luther may well have feared that he would be blamed for the peasant revolt, and that any violence done in the name of reform would
tarnish his ideas and hurt the reforming process. This was not a mis-
placed concern, for many at the time did see a connection.¹⁰ The Catholic poetess and Antwerp schoolmistress Anna Bijns (1493–1575), for
example, expressly tied Luther's teachings to both the revolution and
its horrible aftermath in her poem "On Luther and the Peasants."

> Luther's evil tongue
> Wags at Pope and Emperor alike,
> Teaches subjects revolt against their betters,
> Spreads defamatory libel of kings and princes,
> Flings filth at church lords just the same.

---

9. See Luther, *Against the Robbing and Murdering Hordes of Peasants*, below.

10. See Mark U. Edwards, *Printing, Propaganda and Martin Luther* (Minneapolis, 1994), 149–62.

Luther through his actions
Sent two hundred thousand peasants to their graves.
Blood of men and women freely flowed, with
Water and fire curbing his heretic's views.
So, he has butchered both the soul and the body.

If Luther had kept his tongue behind his teeth,
For such cruel action there'd surely be no need.
And now he plans to wash it off his hands
As Pilate did with our Savior's death.[11]

Despite such criticism, however, and despite disillusionment among the peasantry, Luther's Reformation was ultimately successful, and his alliance with the princes is often seen by historians as a leading factor. From now on, these secular rulers would be the strongest impetus for reform within the empire. This did not upset Luther, for he had always feared popular unrest and social disorder, and he despaired both at the willingness of the common people to follow charismatic fanatics and at their ignorance on the proper meaning of Scripture. After the war, therefore, Luther decided that rulers should have the oversight of external church order within their territories so they could forestall future problems and "repress outward abominations." This elevation of the power of territorial princes over their own churches was something many of them would find extremely appealing, as was Luther's acceptance of their seizure of former Catholic Church lands and properties. Such princely authority was also given legal status at the 1526 imperial diet at Speyer, which granted each imperial ruler the right to choose whether to allow or suppress Lutheran doctrine within his borders.

---

11. Kristiaan P. G. Aercke, "Germanic Sappho: Anna Bijns," in *Women Writers of the Renaissance and Reformation*, edited by Katerina M. Wilson (Athens, GA: University of Georgia Press, 1987), 365–97.

Thomas Müntzer, *Highly Provoked Defense*[1]

The following document was written by Müntzer in response to Luther's Letter to the Princes of Saxony against the Rebellious Spirit at Allstedt (July 1524). He composed it sometime in late 1524, most likely shortly after his forced flight into exile. Müntzer quite correctly saw Luther's hand in his dismissal from Allstedt, and his bitterness against his former friend is obvious throughout, especially toward the end of the document, which in parts disintegrates into almost incoherent rage and invective (most of which I have excluded here). In addition to personal attacks, Müntzer also strongly criticizes Luther's support for the princes, whom Müntzer sees as godless, false Christians bent on oppressing and extorting taxes, rents, and feudal dues from the long-suffering peasants and humble townsfolk. The politics of the day are thus clear here, and one can easily see the early rumblings of the Peasants' War in Müntzer's strong support for the demands of the common people and suggestion that rebellion may be both necessary and justified. In this pamphlet Müntzer also defends his own theological positions against Luther's attacks, stressing the importance of the living Word or Spirit of God working within Christians, and reiterating his long-standing understanding of the importance of both divine grace and law, both faith and works. Luther, he argues, is blind to this truth, corrupted by his worldly desire for honors, insistent on the literal word of Scripture, and unwilling to accept either the Spirit of God or the justifying role of God's law. Note that Müntzer

---

1. Thomas Müntzer, *Hoch verursachte Schutzrede / und antwwort/ wider das Gaistloße Sanfft// lebende fleysch zu Wittenberg/ welches// mit verkaerter weyse / durch den // Diepstal der heiligen Schrift // die erbermdliche Chri=// stenheit / also gätz// jaemerliche// besudelt// hat.// Thomas Müntzer// Alstedter* (Nuremberg: Hieronymus Höltzel, 1524). This pamphlet was suppressed by the authorities in Nuremberg shortly after publication in December 1524, and few copies survive. The translation here is based on the copy held at the Bayerische Staatsbibliothek München (Sigel: 12), Polem. 31.33y. See also Günther Franz, ed., *Thomas Müntzer: Schriften und Briefe, Kritische Gesamtausgabe* (Gütersloh: Gerd Mohn, 1968), 321–43; Manfred Bensing and Bernd Rüdiger, eds., *Thomas Müntzer: Politische Schriften, Manifeste, Briefe* (Leipzig: Bibliographisches Institut, 1973), 140–62.

*openly compares himself here to the crucified Christ, suffering and per-
secuted, and paints Luther as no better, and in fact much worse, than
the Jewish scribes who rejected Christ and His message. It is interesting
to note as well that although Müntzer and John Fisher were on opposite
sides in the Reformation era, both criticized Luther for what they saw
as his misuse of Scripture and for his failure to admit the Spirit of God.*

* * *

Highly Provoked Defense and Answer against the Spiritless, Soft-Living Flesh at Wittenberg[2] Who, in a Perverse Manner and through the Theft of the Holy Scripture, Has Most Miserably Defiled Wretched Christendom. Thomas Müntzer of Allstedt.

From the cave of Elijah, whose severity spares no one (3 Kings 18,[3] Matt.
17:10–12, Luke 1:17, Rev. 11:3–6). In the year 1524.

*O God, rescue me from the false accusations of men so that I may keep
Your commandments and may announce the truth concealed within
Your Son, lest the cunning tricks of the wicked further persevere.*[4]

To the most illustrious, firstborn prince and almighty Lord Jesus
Christ, the benevolent king of all kings, the brave duke of all believers,
my most gracious Lord and true protector, and to His distressed only
bride, poor Christendom.

---

2. Martin Luther. By "Spiritless" Müntzer means "without the Holy Spirit."
3. See instead 3 Kings 19:9–10. All biblical citations shown are given in the
original text, though where practical I have clarified them by giving verse numbers (which Müntzer does not include), and have standardized them to reflect the
most common modern-English naming conventions. Note that here and throughout Müntzer uses the numbering of the books of the Bible as given in the Latin
Vulgate, which was the most common translation of the Bible used in the Middle
Ages (and which had the same enumeration as the older Greek Septuagint). Most
later Protestant bibles use instead the numbering found in the Hebrew-language
Masoretic Text. Thus in Protestant Bibles this would be 1 Kings 19:9–10.
4. This brief prayer is in Latin, unlike the rest of the text.

All praise, fame, honor and dignity, title, and all glory are Yours alone, You eternal Son of God (Phil. 2:9–11), for Your Holy Spirit has always had the fate to seem to those merciless lions, the scribes, that He is the most terrible devil (John 8:48), even though You have had Him without measure from the beginning (John 3:34), and all the chosen have received Him from Your abundance (John 1:16), and He thus lives within them (1 Cor. 3:16, 1 Cor. 6:19, 2 Cor. 1:22, Eph. 1:13, Ps. 5:12⁵). You give Him to all who have run to meet You, according to the measure of their faith (Eph. 4:7, Ps. 67:18–19⁶). And whoever does not have Him, so that he can give an infallible testimony of His Spirit, does not belong to You, Christ (Rom. 8:9). You have the invincible testimony (Ps. 92:5⁷).

For this reason it is no great wonder that the most ambitious scribe, Doctor Liar,⁸ becomes a more haughty fool every day, cloaking himself with Your Holy Scripture and availing himself of it in the most deceptive manner, without any mortal injury to his own fame and comfort. First and foremost, and as if he had gained Your judgment (through You, the gates of truth), he will have nothing to do with You (Isa. 58:2–3), and so is bold to Your face and fundamentally despises Your true Spirit. He declares himself here clearly and irrevocably in that, out of a raging envy and through the most bitter hate, and without any honest, truthful cause, he makes me—who is Your vested member and within You—a laughingstock in front of his derisive, mocking, and most ferocious associates. And, as an irreparable offense against me, he vilifies me as a Satan or devil before the simple people, and, with his perverse, blasphemous judgment, reviles and mocks me.⁹

But in You I am delighted, and I am fully satisfied through Your mild consolation, for as You stated most pleasantly to Your dear friends in Matthew 10:24: "The disciple is not above the master." Since

---

5. Ps. 5:11 in the Masoretic Text.

6. Ps. 68:18–19 in the Masoretic Text. See also Ps. 67/68:10–12.

7. Ps. 93:5 in the Masoretic Text.

8. Martin Luther. Here Müntzer plays on the similarity between Luther's name and the German word for liar, *Lügner*.

9. Here he is referring to Luther's *Letter to the Princes of Saxony against the Rebellious Spirit at Allstedt* (1524).

they have blasphemously called You Beelzebub—who are an innocent duke and comforting Savior—how much more will they attack me, Your undaunted foot soldier, after I have followed Your voice (John 10:3–5) and spoken out against that flattering scoundrel at Wittenberg?[10] Indeed, things must happen in this way, if one will not allow the soft-living know-it-alls, with their contrived faith and Pharisaical deceits, to be seen as right, but will ensure that their fame and grandeur collapse. You too were unable to gain the respect of those of Your time. They let themselves think that they were more learned than You and Your disciples. Indeed, with their literalistic presumption, they were surely more learned than Doctor Mockery[11] could ever be. Even if they had sufficient reputation and fame throughout the world, it still was not right for them to use their intellect to proceed against You, or to wish to prove You wrong with clear Scripture, just as they reproached Nicodemus (John 7:50–52) and spoke of the Sabbath (John 5:9–10, 5:16–18, 9:16). They threw the entire Scripture against You, going to extremes and arguing that You should and must die because You freely confessed that You were the Son of God, born of the eternal Father, just as we are born of Your Spirit. Therefore they said: "We have a law, according to which He must die!" For they stretched the text (Deut. 13:1–5, 18:20) to cover You, and then wished to look no further into it, exactly as the cunning Scripture-thief[12] now does with me. When Scripture is the most revealing, he mocks it with fervent enviousness and calls the Spirit of God a devil.

The whole of Holy Scripture speaks of nothing but the crucified Son of God (as all creatures also proclaim), and for this reason He Himself, to introduce His ministry, also began with Moses and proceeded through all the prophets, thus showing how He must suffer and enter into the glory of His Father. This is clearly described in Luke, in the last chapter.[13] And Paul also said that he could do no other than preach Christ, crucified (1 Cor. 1:23). For after he had researched the law of

---

10. Luther.

11. Luther. Again Müntzer plays with Luther's name, calling him here by the Latin word *Ludibrii* or "Mockery."

12. Luther.

13. Luke 24:25–27, 44–46.

God more deeply than any of his associates (Gal. 1:14–16), he could find within it nothing but the suffering Son of God, who said that He was not come to destroy the law or to tear up the covenant of God, but rather to complete, explain, and fulfill it (Matt. 5:17–18).

The hateful scribes refused to recognize any of this, for they did not study the Scriptures with their entire hearts and spirits, as they ought (Ps. 118:2, 34)[14] and as Christ also commanded them (John 5:39). They were taught from it like monkeys who wanted to imitate a cobbler's shoemaking, but only spoiled the leather. And why? They wanted to embrace the consolation of the Holy Spirit, yet, due to their heart's sadness, for their entire lives it never reached deep within them, as it ought. It should be otherwise: the true light should enlighten in the darkness, and thereby give us the power to be children of God, as is clearly described in Psalm 54:2–9, 22, Psalm 62,[15] and John 1:4–9.

So if Christ is accepted only through the testimony of the old and new covenants[16] of God, and preached without a revelation of the Spirit, then a much worse impediment and monkey game results than that caused by the Jews and heathens. It is now clear for everyone to see that modern scribes do only what the Pharisees did long ago: they boast that they understand the Holy Scripture, cover every book with writing and ink, and babble more and more: "Believe, believe!" And yet they deny the origin of faith, mock the Spirit of God, and really believe nothing at all, as you see. None of them will preach unless he has been paid forty or fifty gulden;[17] indeed, the best of them want more than a hundred or two hundred gulden. Thus they fulfill the prophesy given in Micah 3:11: "The priests preach for the sake of money." And they want to have peace and good comforts and the greatest privilege on earth. And still they think to boast that they understand the source of faith, although in the very greatest contradiction they actually thwart it, which is why they use the cover of the Holy Scripture to vilify the true Spirit as a fallacious spirit and as Satan. This is just what befell Christ,

---

14. Ps. 119:2, 34 in the Masoretic Text.
15. Ps. 55:2–9, 22 and Ps. 63 in the Masoretic Text.
16. The Old and New Testaments.
17. A gold coin.

as by His innocence He announced the will of His Father, something that was much too lofty and distasteful for the scribes (John 5:16–19, 6:38–42).

You will find that nothing has changed up to the current day. When the godless are hemmed in by the law, they say with great levity: "Ha, it is abolished!" However, when it is properly explained to them how the law is written in the heart (2 Cor. 3:2–3), and how one must pay attention to its instructions in order to behold the real paths to the source of faith (Ps. 36:23, 31–32),[18] then the godless assault the just, propounding Paul with such a foolish understanding that even children would see it as a puppet show (Ps. 63).[19] Luther still wants to be the cleverest man on earth, and boasts that he has no equal. Moreover, he calls all the poor people fanatics and refuses to listen whenever one speaks or reads the word "Spirit." He has to shake his clever head, for the devil does not want to hear (Prov. 18:1–3). So when one speaks to him about the beginning of faith, one is driven out. Thus he resorts to deception (2 Cor. 11:13–15). In the highest register of the musicians, the double octave, he sings from Paul in Romans 12:16 that "one should not concern oneself with high things, but be in agreement with the lowly." Such porridge tastes good to him, just as it is, for he dreads soup for breakfast.[20] He says one should simply believe and does not see what this requires. That is why Solomon said of one such person that he was a buffoon, as is written in Proverbs 24:7: "The wisdom of God is much too high for the fool."

Like Moses, Christ began with the source of faith, and explained the law from beginning to end. That is why he said: "I am the light of the world."[21] His preaching was so truthful and so very well composed that He captured the human reason of even the godless, as the evangelist Matthew described in chapter 13:54, and Luke also indicated in chapter 2:47. But since Christ's teaching was too lofty for them[22] and His

---

18. Ps. 37:23, 31–32 in the Masoretic Text.

19. Ps. 64 in the Masoretic Text.

20. In other words, Luther prefers the thick porridge created by his misuse of the Scriptures and fears the clear broth of Scripture properly understood.

21. John 8:12.

22. The scribes and the Pharisees. See John 8:48.

person and life too humble, they became annoyed with Him and His teaching and said to His face that He was a Samaritan and possessed by the devil. For their judgment was made according to the flesh, which delights the devil himself, and it had to be blurted out, for they did not dare to displease the world, which appreciates a Brother Soft Life[23] (Job 28:12–13). Everything they did was designed so that they pleased the world (Matt. 6:1–5, 23:5–7).[24]

The godless flesh at Wittenberg[25] does the same to me, now that I seek the purity of the divine law from the beginning of the Bible and the ordinances of its first chapter (Ps. 18:7–14),[26] and explain how all its judgments show the fulfillment of the Spirit of the fear of God (Isa. 11:1–3). Furthermore, I will not allow his perverse way of using the new covenant[27] of God without explaining divine commandments and the origin of faith, which one can explore only after the punishment of the Holy Spirit (John 16:8). For only after one has knowledge of the law does the Spirit punish unbelief, an unbelief no one recognizes in himself unless he has first confirmed it in his heart as intensely as the most unbelieving heathen. Thus from the beginning, all of the elect have recognized their unbelief through the practice of the law (Rom. 2:12, 7:6–7).[28] I resolve that Christ with all of His members[29] is fulfiller of the law (Ps. 18),[30] for the will of God and His work must be thoroughly carried out by observance of the law (Ps. 1:1–2, Rom.

---

23. I.e., someone like Luther, who had been a monk, and whom Müntzer often criticizes for desiring worldly comforts and honors, rather than wisdom.

24. Here Müntzer is criticizing Luther specifically by suggesting that his judgments (like those of Jesus' critics) are based on his worldly desires for wealth and prestige, not on true faith or the Holy Spirit, and that this leads Luther to try to flatter and win the approval of secular authorities.

25. Luther.

26. Ps. 19:8–15 in the Masoretic Text.

27. The New Testament.

28. Note that while Luther argues that the purpose of the law is to show us our sinfulness and dependence on God's grace, Müntzer argues that the law shows us our lack of belief, which can only be converted to belief by the chastisement of the Holy Spirit and fulfillment of the law.

29. I.e., the true followers of Christ.

30. Ps. 19 in the Masoretic Text.

12:2). Otherwise no one would be able to distinguish faith from unbelief except in a contrived way, like the Jews did with their Sabbath and Scripture, without ever examining the foundations of their faith. I have done nothing to the treacherous raven[31] (which Noah let fly from the ark as a sign) except to brandish my feathers like a simple dove,[32] cover them with silver that has been cleansed seven times, and have my back be gilded (Ps. 67:14),[33] and I have flown over and despised the carrion on which he gladly perches. For I will let the whole world know that he acts hypocritically toward the godless rogues[34]—as you can see in the booklet[35] he wrote against me—and wishes, in short, to defend them. From this it is then clearly evident that Doctor Liar does not dwell in the house of God (Ps. 14).[36] Thus he does not despise the godless; instead, for the sake of the godless, he rebukes many God-fearing people as devils and rebellious spirits. The black raven knows this well. He pecks the eyes from the head of a pig in order to turn it into carrion, just as Luther blinds the pleasure-loving people.[37] Thus he is tame, sated as he is on honors and goods and especially on the greatest titles.[38]

The Jews wanted Christ slandered and put to shame on all sides, just as Luther now does to me. I preach about the seriousness of the law, and how the law's punishment of spiritless transgressors is not abolished (even if they are rulers), but should instead be executed with the greatest seriousness, and in response he fiercely vilifies me and sets before me the benevolence of the Son of God and of His beloved

---

31. Luther.

32. Here Müntzer compares Luther and himself to the two birds released by Noah from the ark, the raven and the dove. See Genesis 8:8–12.

33. Ps. 68:13 in the Masoretic text.

34. The princes of Saxony.

35. Luther's *Letter to the Princes of Saxony* (1524).

36. Ps. 15 in the Masoretic text.

37. The princes.

38. A somewhat complicated metaphor. Here Luther is the raven and the princes are the pig, and Luther turns the princes toward unbelief (as the raven turns the pig into carrion) while taking from them their honors and titles (as the raven pecks out and eats the pig's eyes).

friends. But Paul instructed his disciple Timothy, and through him all
pastors, to preach this to the people (1 Tim. 1:8–11). He said clearly
that the law's punishment should assail all those who fight and strive
against sound teachings, which no one can deny. This lucid clear judgment is contained in Deuteronomy 13:6–11, and Paul also pronounces
it over the unchaste transgressors in 1 Corinthians 5:1–5.

I have had this message printed exactly as I preached it before the
princes of Saxony.[39] Without any guile I indicated to them the sword
mentioned in Scripture, stating that they should use it in order to
block the emergence of a revolt. In short, transgression must be pun-
ished; neither great nor small can get away with it (Num. 25:4). Nevertheless, Father Pussyfoot[40] comes along—O that tame fellow!—and
says I wish to cause a rebellion, which he surmised from my letter to
the miners.[41] He mentions only that one part, but is silent on the most
decisive part: how I clearly explained to the princes that the entire community wields the power of the sword, as well as the keys for remit-
ting sin.[42] And from the texts of Daniel 7:27, Revelation 6:15–17,
Romans 13:1, and 1 Kings 8:1–2,[43] I noted that princes are not lords
of the sword but servants of it. They should not do whatever pleases
them, they should do right (Deut. 17:18–20). Therefore it is a good
old custom that the people must be present whenever a judgment is
to be carried out against someone according to the law of God (Num.
15:35). But why? Because if the authorities wish to pervert their judgment[44] (Isa. 10:1–2), the Christians present should deny it and not
tolerate it. For God demands accountability for the spilling of innocent
blood (Ps. 78:10).[45] It is the greatest abomination on earth that no one

---

39. Müntzer's *Sermon to the Princes* (1524).

40. Luther.

41. A letter of Müntzer's directed to some miners that advocated extreme violence. The letter does not survive.

42. The power of the sword was claimed by rulers, the power of the keys to the
kingdom of heaven was claimed by the Catholic Church, based on Matt. 16:17–19.

43. See also 1 Sam. 8:7.

44. By making laws or judgments hostile to the poor, the needy, widows, and
orphans.

45. Ps. 79:10 in the Masoretic text.

will embrace the misery of the needy, while the great do whatever they wish, as is described in Job 41.

The poor flatterer[46] wants to cloak himself with the contrived benevolence of Christ, contrary to the text of Paul (1 Tim. 1:7–11). In his book about trade,[47] however, he says that the princes should confidently go along with thieves and robbers. But in the same book he is silent about the source of all theft. He is a herald who wishes to earn thanks for approving the shedding of the people's blood for the sake of temporal goods, which God certainly did not intend or command. Observe the dregs of usury, theft, and robbery that are our lords and princes, who take all creatures as their property; the fish in the water, the birds in the air, the plants in the earth must all be theirs (Isa. 5:8). Then, in addition, they have the law of God sent out among the poor and say: "God has commanded: you shall not steal." But this does not serve their interests, so they have all men plundered and fleeced: the poor plowman, craftsman, and everyone who lives (Mic. 3:2–4). Yet as soon as one of these men takes the smallest thing, he must hang. To this Doctor Liar says "Amen." The lords themselves make the poor man their enemy. They do not wish to do away with the source of the rebellion, so how can things be improved in the long run? If I say this, I must be rebellious. So be it! . . .

The devil uses quite cunning frauds in order to oppose Christ and His people (2 Cor. 6:14, 11:14–15): sometimes with flattering benevolence, as Luther does when he defends the godless using the words of Christ; sometimes with fierce severity, applying his pernicious justice for the sake of temporal goods. Yet the finger of Christ, the Holy Spirit (2 Cor. 3:3), does not imprint such fierceness on the friendly severity of the law, and the crucified Son of God, out of the most severe benevolence, discloses the divine will through a comparison of both severity and benevolence (1 Cor. 2). But Luther despises the law of the fathers, uses that most precious treasure, the benevolence of Christ, in order to act hypocritically, and uses the forbearance of the Son in order to disgrace the Father and the severity of His law (John 15:10, 16:15).

---

46. Luther.
47. Luther, *On Trade and Usury* (1524).

He thus despises the distinction the Holy Spirit makes between the two[48] and so corrupts the one with the other. Thus almost no judgment remains on earth (Jer. 5:31) and it seems that Christ is forbearing only so that godless Christians may torment their brothers. . . .

Shame on you, Luther, you arch-knave! Will you insinuate yourself with an erring world (Luke 9:25), and will you justify all mankind? You know well, however, whom you shall malign: the poor monks and priests and merchants; they cannot defend themselves, thus you can easily vilify them. But you say no one should judge the godless rulers, even if they tread Christ underfoot. To satisfy the peasants, you wrote that the princes will be shattered through the word of God. And you say in your commentary on the recent imperial mandate: "The princes will be toppled from their thrones."[49] Yet you still esteem them as greater than merchants. You should tweak the noses of your princes too. They have deserved it much more perhaps than the others. Which of their rents, extortions, etc., have they given up? Although you have chastised the princes, you can easily give them renewed courage, you new pope, by giving them monasteries and churches.[50] Then they will be satisfied with you. This is what I would advise you! Otherwise the peasants may chime in! . . .

I speak of the divine word with its manifold treasures (Col. 2:3), which Moses offers to teach in Deuteronomy 30:11–14 and Paul in Romans 10:8. Psalm 84:9[51] also says that the word shall be heard by those who are converted with their entire heart and who strive to find in the teaching of the Spirit all judgments about the mercy and righteousness of God. You, however, deny the true word and present only its semblance to the world. You coarsely make yourself into an arch-devil, for without any understanding you use the text of Isaiah[52] to make God the cause of evil. Is that not the most terrible punishment

---

48. The mercy of Christ and the law of God the Father.

49. Luther used Luke 1:52 to warn the princes in his *Two Discordant and Despicable Imperial Mandates Concerning Martin Luther* (1524).

50. Luther supported secular princes' confiscation of ecclesiastical properties in their territories.

51. Ps. 85:9 in the Masoretic text.

52. Isa. 40:2–8.

of God on you? You remain blinded, and yet you want to be the leader of the world's blind. You also want to lay the blame on God for the fact that you are a poor sinner and a poisonous little worm with your crappy humility. This is what you have constructed out of your fanciful understanding of your Augustine.[53] It is truly a blasphemous thing to despise so boldly the free will of mankind! . . .

O Doctor Liar, you treacherous fox, through your lies you have saddened the heart of the righteous, whom God has not afflicted. Thereby you have strengthened the power of the godless evildoers, so that they remain set on their old paths. Thus you will suffer the same fate as a captured fox. The people will be free, and God alone will be lord over them!

---

53. St. Augustine of Hippo (354–430), was perhaps the most influential theologian and church father in the history of Western Christendom. Luther's teachings on free will, works, and salvation were based in large part on his reading of Augustine.

Martin Luther, *Against the Robbing and Murdering Hordes of Peasants*[1]

Against the Rioting Peasants *is one of Luther's harshest writings, and one that even he felt uneasy about afterward. It was written in response to the extreme violence of the German Peasants' War, and most likely was sparked by the news in April 1525 of the murders by rebellious peasants of the count of Helfenstein and his men in the city of Weinsberg. Although Luther had earlier offered a much more balanced admonition to both the peasants and the nobility to come to peace and resolve their issues without violence, here he has clearly chosen sides. Whether the nobles oppressed the peasants or not, whether they supported the gospel or not, he argued, the peasants by revolting were doing the work of the devil and should be killed without mercy. In return, the nobles could be assured that they were doing God's work. Luther's sudden turn toward violence, which he had earlier and quite specifically disavowed, is hard to explain. Clearly he was appalled by the bloodshed that resulted from the peasants' uprising, but he was also socially conservative, and the peasants' demands for economic and social equality seemed to him both wrong and unbiblical. Furthermore, this document strongly suggests that Luther was concerned that the peasants were misusing his ideas. Their argument that they were only acting on the authority of Scripture, and only seeking Christian freedom, must have seemed to him like a betrayal and perversion of his teachings. Even worse, of course, was the fear that he might then be blamed for their violence and social disruption.*

* * *

---

1. This translation is based on the German text given in Martin Luther, *D. Martin Luthers Werke: Kritische Gesamtausgabe*, vol. 18 (Weimar, 1908), 357–63.

Against the Rioting Peasants

In my former booklet[2] I did not have reason to judge the peasants, since they had offered to be put right and to be better instructed; for as Christ commanded, one should not judge (Matt. 7).[3] But before I could even turn around, out they went and acted with their fists, forgetting their offer, robbing and killing and behaving like crazed dogs. From this one can easily see what they had in their false minds, and that the things they proposed in the *Twelve Articles*[4] under the name of the gospel were pure lies. In short, they are doing nothing but the devil's work, and particularly the work of the arch-devil who reigns at Mühlhausen[5] and perpetrates nothing but robbery, murder, and bloodshed; as Christ then says of him in John 8: "he was a murderer from the beginning."[6] Now since such peasants and wretched people have let themselves become ensnared, and so do otherwise than they have said, I too must write otherwise of them; first to place their sins before their eyes, as God orders Isaiah and Ezekiel, in case some would see themselves for what they are; and then to instruct the secular authorities on how they should conduct themselves in this matter.

These peasants have brought upon themselves three horrible sins against God and man, by which they have abundantly earned death in body and soul. First, they have sworn loyalty and homage to their governing authorities and promised to be submissive and obedient,[7] which is something God has commanded, for He says: "Render unto Caesar the things that are Caesar's;"[8] and in Romans 13: "Let every man be subject to the governing authorities, etc."[9] Because, however, they are willfully and recklessly breaking this obedience and also

---

2. Luther's 1525 *Admonition to Peace*.

3. Matt. 7:1.

4. The *Twelve Articles* of the peasants of Swabia (1525).

5. Thomas Müntzer.

6. John 8:44.

7. This was a standard oath, made in God's name, that all residents of a place gave to their local lord or ruler on his ascension to the throne.

8. Luke 20:25.

9. Rom. 13:1.

setting themselves against their lords, they have thereby forfeited their bodies and souls, just as disloyal, perjuring, mendacious, disobedient knaves and villains are wont to do. Thus St. Paul, in Romans 13, also offers such a verdict of them: "Whoever resists the power . . . he shall bring judgment upon himself."[10] In the end this saying will also affect the peasants, whether sooner or later, for God wants loyalty and duty upheld.

Second, they are causing a rebellion and recklessly robbing and plundering monasteries and castles that are not theirs; thus as highwaymen and murderers alone they are culpable a second time for death in body and soul. Furthermore, a man proven to be rebellious is already an outlaw to God and the emperor, so that the first man who can and may slay him does so legally and properly.[11] For against an open rebel every man is both judge and executioner, just as when a fire breaks out, whoever can first extinguish it is the best person to do so. For rebellion is not ordinary murder, but is like a great fire that inflames and devastates a land. Thus rebellion brings with it a land full of murder and bloodshed, it makes widows and orphans, and it upends everything like the greatest disaster. Therefore whoever can, should now strike, slay, and stab, secretly or openly, and consider that there can be nothing more poisonous, damaging, and devilish than a rebellious man. It is just like when one must club dead a mad dog; if you do not smite him, he will smite you—and a whole land with you.

Third, they cloak such terrible, horrible sin with the gospel, call themselves Christian brethren, swear oaths and homage, and force the people to uphold such abominations along with them. Thereby they become the greatest blasphemers of God and defilers of His holy name, and so serve the devil under the pretext of the gospel. From this they have earned death in body and soul ten times over, for I have never heard of more hideous sins. And I also think that the devil senses the coming of Judgment Day, so that he undertakes such an unheard-of action, as if he is saying: "It is the last, therefore it shall be the worst; I will stir up the

---

10. Rom. 13:2.

11. Note that Luther himself was proclaimed an outlaw by Emperor Charles V in May 1521, after the Diet of Worms.

dregs and rip out the very bottom."[12] May God oppose him! See what a mighty prince the devil is, how he has the world in his hands and can throw it into confusion. He can so quickly entrap, mislead, blind, and make obstinate and rebellious so many thousands of peasants, and can do with them whatever his raging fury intends.

It also does not help the peasants that they pretend that, according to Genesis 1 and 2, all things were created free and in common, and that we have all alike been baptized. For Moses neither appears in nor pertains to the New Testament; rather there stands our master, Christ, who subjects us, along with our bodies and possessions, to the emperor and worldly law, for He says: "Render unto Caesar the things that are Caesar's."[13] And Paul also says to all baptized Christians in Romans 12: "Let every man be subject to the governing authorities."[14] And Peter: "Be subject to every ordinance of man."[15] We are required to live by this teaching of Christ, for our Father in heaven commanded and said: "This is My beloved Son. . . . Listen to Him."[16] For baptism does not make one free in body and possessions, but in soul; and the gospel does not make possessions common, except only for those who, willingly and on their own initiative, imitate the apostles and disciples in Acts 4. These did not demand, as our senseless peasants rant, that the possessions of others—of a Pilate and Herod—be in common, but only their own possessions. Our peasants, however, want to have other men's possessions in common, and to keep their own possessions for themselves. These seem to me fine Christians! I think that there is not a devil left in hell, for they have all entered into the peasants. Their raging is limitless and beyond all measure.

---

12. An old saying in German that literally means destroying a barrel or vat of soured or poor-quality beer by knocking or ripping out its bottom, thereby making the liquid spill out so greedy merchants are unable to sell it to unsuspecting customers. Figuratively this means making something unusable or destroying it—in this case, the world. For Luther's use of this saying, see Ernst Thiele, *Luthers Sprichwörtersammlung* (Weimar: H. Böhlaus Nachfolger, 1900), 305–6.

13. Luke 20:25.

14. Rom. 13:1.

15. 1 Pet. 2:13.

16. Matt. 17:5.

Because the peasants have now brought both God and man down upon themselves, are so abundantly responsible for death in both body and soul, and neither accept nor await any law but rampage ever on, I must here instruct the secular authorities on how they should proceed in this matter in good conscience. First, I will not oppose a ruler, even one who does not tolerate the gospel,[17] who can and will smite and punish such peasants without first appealing to law and justice. For he has every right, since the peasants are no longer battling for the gospel, but have publicly become disloyal, perjuring, disobedient, and rebellious murderers, robbers, and blasphemers of God, whom even a heathenish ruler has the right and power to punish. Indeed, it is his responsibility to punish such knaves, for it is for this reason that he wields the sword and is the minister of God over those who do evil (Rom. 13).[18]

But the ruler who is Christian and tolerates the gospel, and so on this account the peasants have no appearance of a case against him, should here proceed with fear. First, he should entrust the matter to God and recognize that we have surely deserved this, also dreading that perhaps God thus aroused the devil for the common punishment of Germany. Thereafter, he should humbly beg for help against the devil, for "we battle here not solely against flesh and blood, but against . . . spiritual wickedness in the air,"[19] which must be attacked with prayer. Now, when his heart is so directed to God that he will allow His divine will to be done (whether God wishes to have him be prince and lord, or not), he should offer law and justice in abundance to the mad peasants, even though they are unworthy. Thereafter, should this not help, he should quickly take up the sword.

For a prince and lord must now consider that he is God's minister and the servant of His wrath (Rom. 13),[20] to whom it is commanded to wield the sword over such knaves. And if he does not punish and oppose them and does not fulfill his office, he sins as greatly against God as does a man who has not been commanded to wield the sword and yet murders. For where he is able to but does not punish, even

---

17. In other words, is not a follower of Luther's teachings.
18. Rom. 13:4.
19. Eph. 6:12.
20. Rom. 13:4.

by means of murder or bloodshed, he is then responsible for all the murder and evil that such knaves commit; for by wantonly declining God's divine commandment, he permits such knaves to practice their wickedness—even though he can oppose it and is responsible for it. Therefore now is not the time to sleep; nor is either patience or compassion valid. Now is the time of the sword and of wrath, not of mercy.

Thus the ruler should now press on confidently and strike them down with good conscience, so long as the blood beats within him. For here is his advantage: the peasants have evil consciences and an unjust cause, and whatever peasants are slain over this are lost in body and soul and are eternally the devil's. But the ruler has a good conscience and a just cause, and can say to God with full certainty in his heart: "Behold, my God, You have appointed me prince or lord, this I cannot doubt; and You have commanded me to wield the sword against evildoers (Rom. 13).[21] It is Your word, and it cannot lie, so I must fulfill my office or lose Your grace. It is also clear, before You and the world, that these peasants have manifoldly earned death and have been commended to me for punishment. If You now wish me to be killed by them, and allow my authority to be taken from me and be destroyed, well then: let Your will be done. I shall indeed die and be destroyed according to Your divine command and word, and shall be found in obedience to Your commandment and my office. Therefore I will punish and smite, so long as blood beats within me. You will direct things and make them right."

Thus it may be that whoever is slain fighting on the side of the authorities would be a true martyr to God, if he fights with a conscience like that described above; for he proceeds in obedience to the divine word. On the other hand, whoever dies fighting on the side of the peasants is one who will eternally burn in hell; for he wields the sword against God's word and obedience and is the devil's arm. And even if it should happen that the peasants gain the upper hand (God forbid!)—for to God all things are possible, and we do not know if, in advance of the Final Judgment, which is not far off, it may be His will to destroy all order and authority through the devil, and to toss the world into a devastated heap—nevertheless, those who are found with their sword of office can die certain and fail with good conscience, and

---

21. Rom. 13:4.

can leave the worldly kingdom to the devil and take in exchange the eternal kingdom. Such strange times these are, when a prince can earn heaven with bloodshed sooner than another can with prayer.

Finally, there is still one thing that should by rights move the authorities. For the peasants do not let it suffice that they are the devil's own. Instead, they force and urge many pious people to join their devilish league against their wills, and so make these same people participate in all of their wickedness and damnation. For whoever conspires with them also goes to the devil with them and is guilty of all the evil deeds that they commit; although he must act thusly, because he is of such weak faith that he cannot oppose them. Yet a pious Christian should suffer a hundred deaths before he concedes a hairbreadth toward the peasants' cause. O how many further martyrs might yet be created by the bloodthirsty peasants and the prophets of murder! Now the authorities should have pity on such prisoners of the peasants, and if they have no other reason to let loose their swords with confidence against the peasants, and not even to spare their own body and possessions in the process, then this last point would be sufficiently great: one would thereby rescue and help such souls, who are forced by the peasants into such a devilish league and who, against their wills, sin with them so dreadfully that they must be damned. For such souls are truly in purgatory; indeed, they are in the shackles of hell and the devil.

Therefore, dear lords, now release, rescue, help. Take pity on the poor people! Whoever can, now stab, smite, slay. If you should thereby die, good for you; you could never gain a more blessed death. For you die in obedience to the divine word and commandment in Romans 13,[22] and in loving service of your neighbor, rescuing him from the shackles of hell and the devil. So I beg you now, flee from the peasants, whoever is able, as if from the devil himself. Whoever will not flee, I beg that God will enlighten and convert you. For those who will not be converted, however, may God grant that they have no fortune or success. Here every pious Christian says Amen! For I know this prayer is just and good and well pleases God. If anyone thinks it is too harsh, think too that rebellion is intolerable and that the destruction of the world is to be expected at any hour.

---

22. Rom. 13:1–5.

Further Reading

Bainton, Roland Herbert. *Here I Stand*. New York: Abingdon Press, 1950.

Bagchi, David V. N. *Luther's Earliest Opponents: Catholic Controversialists, 1518–1525*. Minneapolis: Augsburg Fortress, 1991.

Baylor, Michael G., ed. *The Radical Reformation*. Cambridge Texts in the History of Political Thought. Cambridge: Cambridge University Press, 1991.

Bireley, Robert. *The Refashioning of Catholicism, 1450–1700: A Reassessment of the Counter Reformation*. Washington, D.C.: Catholic University of America Press, 1999.

Blickle, Peter. *Communal Reformation: The Quest for Salvation in Sixteenth-Century Germany*. Atlantic Highlands, NJ: Humanities Press, 1992.

———. *The Revolution of 1525: The German Peasants' War from a New Perspective*. Baltimore: Johns Hopkins University Press, 1981.

Brecht, Martin. *Martin Luther*. Philadelphia: Fortress Press, 1985.

Cameron, Euan. *The European Reformation*. Oxford: Oxford University Press, 1991.

Cohn, Norman. *The Pursuit of the Millennium: Revolutionary Millenarians and Mystical Anarchists of the Middle Ages*. Oxford: Oxford University Press, 1970.

Dixon, C. Scott. *Contesting the Reformation*. Malden, MA: Wiley-Blackwell, 2012.

———. *The Reformation in Germany*. Oxford: Blackwell Publishers, 2002.

Duffy, Eamon. *The Stripping of the Altars: Traditional Religion in England, 1400–1580*. 2nd ed. New Haven: Yale University Press, 2005.

Edwards, Mark U. *Luther and the False Brethren*. Stanford: Stanford University Press, 1975.

———. *Luther's Last Battles*. Minneapolis: Augsburg Fortress, 2004.

———. *Printing, Propaganda and Martin Luther*. Minneapolis: Augsburg Fortress, 1994.

———. "The Reception of Luther's Understanding of Freedom in the Early Modern Period." *Lutherjahrbuch* 62 (1995):104–20.

Gritsch, Eric W. *Thomas Müntzer: A Tragedy of Errors*. Minneapolis: Augsburg Fortress, 2006.

Haigh, Christopher. *English Reformations: Religion, Politics, and Society Under the Tudors*. Oxford: Oxford University Press, 1993.

Hillerbrand, Hans Joachim. *The Division of Christendom: Christianity in the Sixteenth Century*. Louisville: Westminster John Knox Press, 2007.

Hsia, R. Po-chia. *The World of Catholic Renewal, 1540–1770*. 2nd ed. Cambridge: Cambridge University Press, 2005.

Kittelson, James M. *Luther the Reformer: The Story of the Man and His Career*. Minneapolis: Augsburg Fortress, 2003.

Lindberg, Carter. *The European Reformations*. Oxford: Blackwell, 1996.

————. *The Reformation Theologians: An Introduction to Theology in the Early Modern Period*. The Great Theologians. Oxford: Blackwell, 2002.

Loewenich, Walther Von. *Martin Luther: The Man and His Work*. Minneapolis: Augsburg Fortress, 1986.

Lohse, Bernhard. *Martin Luther: An Introduction to His Life and Work*. Philadelphia: Fortress Press, 1986.

————. *Martin Luther's Theology: Its Historical and Systematic Development*. Minneapolis: Fortress Press, 1999.

Luebke, David, ed. *The Counter-Reformation: The Essential Readings*. Malden, MA: Wiley-Blackwell, 1999.

Lull, Timothy F. *Martin Luther's Basic Theological Writings*. 3rd ed. Minneapolis: Fortress Press, 2012.

MacCulloch, Diarmaid. *The Reformation*. 1st American ed. New York: Viking, 2004.

McGrath, Alister E. *Reformation Thought: An Introduction*. 4th ed. Malden, MA: Wiley-Blackwell, 2012.

Mullett, Michael. *The Catholic Reformation*. London: Routledge, 1999.

Oberman, Heiko A., ed. *Forerunners of the Reformation: The Shape of Late Medieval Thought*. Cambridge: Cambridge University Press, 1966.

————. *Luther: Man Between God and the Devil*. Translated by Eileen Walliser-Schwarzbart. New Haven: Yale University Press, 2006.

Ozment, Steven E. *The Age of Reform (1250–1550): An Intellectual and Religious History of Late Medieval and Reformation Europe*. New Haven: Yale University Press, 1980.

Rublack, Ulinka. *Reformation Europe*. New Approaches to European History, vol. 28. Cambridge: Cambridge University Press, 2005.

Rupp, E. G. and B. Drewery, eds. *Martin Luther*. London: Edward Arnold, 1970.

Scott, Tom. *Thomas Müntzer: Theology and Revolution in the German Reformation*. New York: St. Martin's, 1989.

Scribner, Robert W. *The German Reformation*. 2nd ed. Studies in European History. Houndmills: Palgrave Macmillan, 2003.

Tracy, James D. *Europe's Reformations, 1450–1650*. Critical Issues in History. Lanham: Rowman & Littlefield, 1999.

Wandel, Lee Palmer. *The Reformation: Towards a New History*. 1st ed. Cambridge: Cambridge University Press, 2011.

Williams, George Huntston. *The Radical Reformation*. Kirksville, MO: Truman State University Press, 2000.

Index